DE BESTIIS MARINIS

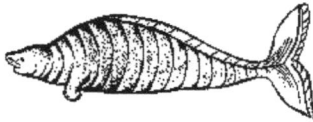

OR,

THE BEASTS OF THE SEA

De bestiis marinis

or,

The Beasts of the Sea

by

Georg Wilhelm Steller

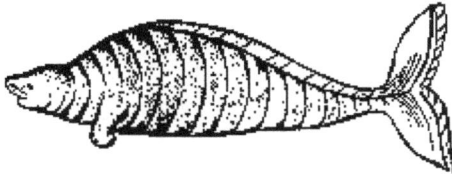

Translated by

Walter Miller

Professor of Classical Philology
Leland Stanford Junior University
and

Jennie Emerson Miller

Transcribed and edited by

Paul Royster

Zea Books
Lincoln, Nebraska 2011

DE BESTIIS MARINIS was published (in Latin) in *Novi Commentarii Academiae Scientiarum Imperialis Petropolitanae, Tom. II, ad annum MDCCXLIX* (Petropoli [St. Petersburg]: Typia Academiae Scientiarum, 1751), pp. 289-398.

This English translation was published in *The Fur Seals and Fur-Seal Islands of the North Pacific Ocean,* edited by David Starr Jordan, Part 3 (Washington: Government Printing Office, 1899), pp. 179-218, as "Part VIII. — The Early History of the Northern Fur Seals."

Zea Books are published by the University of Nebraska-Lincoln Libraries.

ISBN 978-1-60962-010-3

Contents

Translators' Preface

Steller's work, published in 1751 in the memoirs of the Imperial Academy of Sciences in St. Petersburg for the year 1749, is a posthumous publication. The greater part of the work was finished in 1742, and Steller himself died, while on his way from Siberia to St. Petersburg, in November, 1745. He was the naturalist (a volunteer) of the Russian expedition sent out to explore the northwest coast of North America and to ascertain definitely whether it was or was not joined to Asia, and to search for the imaginary island known as Compagnie Land.

The following pages contain a translation of those parts of Steller's report which treat of the Manatee, or sea cow (Vol. II, pp. 289-330), and the natural history of the sea bear (fur seal) (pp. 346-359), sea lion (pp. 361-366), and sea otter (pp. 382-398). The measurements and descriptions of the last three are omitted, inasmuch as they can be made better and with more scientific accuracy in our own times. But as the sea cow is extinct, and as nearly all knowledge of it is to be obtained from Steller's account, that portion of his work is given in full.

Circumstances have combined to render the work of translation difficult; not only is Steller's account written in the zoological Latin of the eighteenth century, but, as printed, it contains errors and omissions due to the fact that it was published after Steller's death, and consequently without revision. Finally, it has been necessary to rely on a type-written copy, the original not being accessible to the translator.*

Thanks are due to President David Starr Jordan and to Professor Oliver Peebles Jenkins for much kind assistance with the technical, scientific, physiological, and anatomical parts of the work.

[W.M. & J.E.M.]

* The Latin original may be seen online at the Niedersaechsische Staats- und Universitaets-bibliothek Goettingen (Goettingen State and University Library) http://www-gdz.sub.uni-goettingen.de/cgi-bin/digbib.cgi? PPN350003793

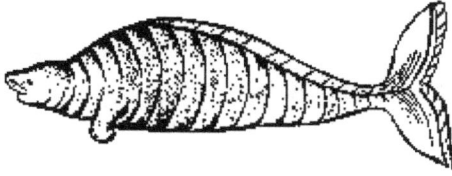

No one who has studied various lands doubts that the vast ocean contains many animals which to-day are unknown, and that there are very many regions in the ocean where the curious and venturesome inquiries of Europeans have not yet penetrated; and so no one has been able to examine their contents. Thus it stands with the animals of the sea as compared with the animals of the land. Some live anywhere and everywhere, and through long association come to vary their species in accordance with differences of climate and food, not only in respect to size and color, but also in respect to the softness and thickness of their hair; but when transferred to a different climate, after a long interval of time they lose again their specific difference and revert to the first. So European horses when transferred to Siberia become perceptibly smaller and hardier; and, on the other hand, when taken to India or China they become so much slighter and smaller that after a lapse of time they form a peculiar species. Yakut cattle when transported to Kamchatka become not only larger, but more prolific; and this is the case also with cattle that are sent to the port of Archangel. With English sheep that are taken to Sweden on account of the excellence of their wool, not only the wool changes after a short time, but also their size. If one did not observe this, it would seem that the species of animals increased gradually in Siberia alone; for example, the squirrels on the Obi are large, and covered with long, ashy gray fur; Obdoric squirrels are one-third smaller, and covered with short but thicker fur; Bargusian squirrels are covered with black, and Werchoian squirrels are mottled with black and ash-colored fur. All this difference, as far as concerns size and thickness of fur, is due to climate, and as far as concerns the color it is due to the food. Where evergreen larches, or, as they are commonly called, spruce and pines, grow, there the fur is a bright, ashy gray; where the larches are deciduous, there they grow with black fur.

Among animals the seal (*phoca*) is the only one which lives not only in every part of the ocean, but in the Baltic Sea, the Caspian Sea, and lakes which have no communication with the sea, as in Lakes Baikal and Oron; it is found everywhere at all times of the year. Notwithstanding, this difference occurs, that the ocean seal (*Phoca oceanica*) is more common and is distinguished in color from all the rest; it is covered with muddy gray fur, and on the back of its body it has a large spot that is chestnut colored and covers one-third of the whole hide.

Now, I divide seals into three varieties on the basis of size. (1.) The largest, which is greater in size than a bull, grows only in the eastern ocean from the degrees 56 to 59 north latitude, and is called by the Kamchatkans "*Lachtak*." (2) Those of medium size are all as large as a tiger, and are marked with many smaller spots. (3) The smallest ones — the ocean seal, for example — are found in the Baltic Sea, as well as in the port of Archangel, in Sweden, Norway, America, and Kamchatka, and in fresh-water lakes. They are monochroüs; that is, of one color; for example, those found in Baikal are of a silvery gray color. If we inquire why this sort of amphibian alone lives in every ocean and lake, I reply, because it lives upon a sort of food which is to be had everywhere in the world, and upon flesh. But the case of the sea cow (*Manatee*) is different. It feeds only upon certain sorts of sea weeds not found everywhere, and on account of the structure of its body can not live everywhere even in shallow places. But the sea otter, although it lives upon crustaceans and shellfish, can not find this sort of food everywhere beneath a certain depth of water on account of its closed *foramen ovale*; and hence it inhabits the rocky, rugged, shallow shoals of America, of the islands in the channel, and of the land of Kamchatka. The sea lion and the sea bear are migratory animals, and seek the recesses of the sea and uninhabited islands in the same way as geese and swans, so that there they may get rid of their fat, copulate, and give birth, and when that is done they return home in the same way as birds.

The amphibious *Bieluga*, a most voracious animal, selects those places where there are long inlets of the sea; they generally wander about very widely, where they can drive the fishes together and devour them more quickly in larger numbers — such places as are at the mouth of the Ud and Ochotsk and the arm of the sea at the mouth of the river Olutora. The walrus, from his love of ease, seeks out desolate and uninhabited places, and because of his fatness selects a cold place in the midst of ice, and because he finds these conditions at any time of the year at the mouth of the river Obi, Yenisee, Lena, and Kolima, and around Cape Tschutschi, he is fond of those regions. The right whale (*balaena*), because it is fond of peace, chooses those parts of the sea less frequented by ships, and since those places are for the most part in the north, whales live there and select those regions for sleep, for giving birth to their young, and for breeding.

Accordingly, the reason why other amphibious animals inhabit not all but only some certain regions of the ocean, must be looked for in the nature of the animals themselves. For some the food that they eat, for others their love of ease, for others still different characteristics fix their boundaries and determine their dwelling-places.

But all sea animals have something, either in appearance or in habits, in common with land animals, on account of which even at first sight they are compared by the common people to these animals, and thus get their names. So the host of natural philosophers talk about bulls, horses, wolves, and, dreaming of allegories, bring in monks and other men. It has seemed to me worth mentioning that Ruthenian sailors when they first saw the manatee called it "*Korova Morskaia,*" (Корова Морская) with exactly the same propriety as the English and Dutch called it a "sea-cow;" "*Sivutcha*" (Сивуча) they called "sea-lion," and "*Kot*" (Кошъ) "sea-bear." Not noticing the criteria offered by nature, they less appropriately called the "sea-otter" "*Bobr Morskoi*" (Бобоъ морской). But all these animals became known only half a century ago; in fact, Marcgraf makes mention of the sea otter, but somewhat briefly and obscurely. The navigator Dampier, a tireless explorer, speaks of the sea lion and the sea bear; and many learned men, and Dampier as well, mention the manatee. But I must admit that the accounts given by the scholars are fragmentary and imperfect and for the most part fabulous and false. Dampier, on the other hand, has by many parasangs* excelled them with a most accurate description, as good as could be expected from an unlearned man.

* *parasang*: ancient Persian unit of distance, estimated at 3.5 miles.

But one must not suppose that these places do not contain more great and wonderful animals that are still unknown, besides those which I shall describe. For if weather, time, and place had favored my desire I should have enriched natural history with many curiosities of that sort, as indeed I desired when I took the risk of this journey to parts so distant and unexplored. Thus, for instance, I describe the traces of a certain unknown animal upon the island of Shumagin, and I insert a sketch of a sea ape, and with this imperfect account I must content myself and others.

In what order I shall next year examine the shores of the sea near the mouth of the river Kolima time will tell. My zeal is fired by those mammoth skeletons and the slight accounts of them. And I do not doubt that the American shores are to become better known to us, and with them this wonderful subject as well. As long as things escape us and perish unknown with our consent, and through our silence are counted as fabulous — things which may be seen with little labor in the very land where we, with all our inquisitiveness, live — it is not strange that these things, which we are prevented from observing by the great sea that lies between, have remained to the present time unknown and unexplored. In the farther confines of Asia and the Russian Empire I learned that the "*Suhac*" of the Scythians was regarded as fabulous. I also learned that in the Desert of Azof, and in that where the Saporozkiensian Cossacks live, the one-horned goat bears the same name — an animal very common and very well known upon their tables. There is likewise a Scythian wolf, black in color, and described by Aristotle as longer than the common wolf but with shorter legs, exceedingly fierce and savage. There is also in the neighborhood of Voronesch and Astracan an animal that barks like a dog. It is sly and bloodthirsty and will attack people lying asleep or steal whatever it can from the household stores. This maybe the hyena of ancient times. And I desire nothing more than that, after I have explored Siberia, the authorities may think well to intrust to me the exploration of the deserts — provided no one else undertakes it; and I hope that if my efforts prove acceptable I may be sent into exile for several years on their account, that I may spend there a long time, which I prophesy will prove but too brief.

The Manatee

The following is a description of the manatee, or, as it is called by the Dutch, *Vacca marina* (sea cow), by the English, "sea cow," and by the Russians, "*Morskaia Korova;*" the description is made from a female killed on the 12th of July, 1742, on Bering Island, which lies in the channel between America and Asia. It had, according to the English scale of measurement, the following dimensions:

	Inches,	tenths
Length from the extremity of the upper lip to the extreme right *cornu* of the caudal fork --------------	296	0
From the extremity of the upper lip to the nares ---------	8	0
From the narial septum (*columna narium*) to the anterior angle of the eye ------------------------------------	13	5
From the anterior angle to the posterior angle of the eye	-- 8	
Distance between the eyes at the anterior angles --------	17	4
Distance between the eyes at the posterior angles -------	22	2
The breadth of the narial septum (*columna narium*) at its base ---	1	5
Height of the nares -------------------------------------	2	5
Breadth of the nares -----------------------------------	2	5
From the extremity of the upper lip to the angle of the mouth (*oris froenum*) ---------------------------	15	5
From the extremity of the upper lip to the shoulder ------	52	0
From the extremity of the upper lip to the opening of the vulva ---------------------------------------	194	0
Length of the vulva -------------------------------------	10	2
Length of the tail from the anal sphincter to the region of the caudal fin -------------------------	75	5
Circumference of the head above the nostrils (*supra nares*) -------------------------------	31	0
Circumference of the head at the eyes ----------------	48	0
Circumference of the neck at the nape (*nucham*) --------	82	0
Height of the end of the snout ----------------------	8	4
Circumference of the body at the shoulders -----------	144	0
The greatest circumference about the middle of the abdomen ---	244	0

The circumference of the tail at the origin (*insertio*) of the fin	56	0
Distance between the extreme points of the caudal fin (this is the breadth of the fin)	78	0
Height of the fin	8	8
The whole length of the inner lip, which is villous and rough, like a brush	5	2
Width of the same	2	5
The width of the exterior upper lip, which stands obliquely to the lower jaw and is covered all over with rather long, white bristles	14	0
Height of the same	10	0
The breadth of the lower lip, which is hairless, black, smooth, and slopes toward the sternum, and is heart-shaped	7	4
Height of the same	6	8
From the lower lip to the sternum	54	0
The diameter of the mouth at the angle (*oris froenum*)	20	4
From the pharynx to the end of the oesophagus	32	0
The width, or rather length, of the stomach	44	0
The whole intestinal tract, from pharynx to anus	5,968	0
And so it is 20 ½ times as long as the whole animal.		
From pudenda to anal sphincter	8	0
Diameter of the trachea below the glottis	4	2
Height ot the heart	22	0
Width of the heart	25	0
Length of the kidneys	32	0
Width of the kidneys	18	0
Length of the tongue	12	0
Width of the tongue	2	5
Length of the nipples	4	0
Width of the humerus	14	5
Length of the ulna	12	2
Length of the skull from nares to occiput	27	0
Width of the occiput	10	5

Description of the External Parts

This animal belongs practically to the sea, and is not amphibious, although some authorities have so narrated; but they have misunderstood the stories of some others who tell of its feeding upon vegetation about the shores of the sea and rivers. But by this was meant not the vegetation of the land, but seaweed that grows out in the water on the shore of the sea. This seemed quite an unwelcome fact (that it fed on seaweed) and most absurd to Celsius Clusius, who had seen a whole hide stuffed with straw; but it is found to be so also in the case of the living beast (strange as it is true), if one will but have regard to its form, movements, and habits.

It is covered with a thick hide, more like unto the bark of an ancient oak than unto the skin of an animal; the manatee's hide is black, mangy, wrinkled, rough, hard, and tough; it is void of hairs, and almost impervious to an ax or to the point of a hook. It is an inch thick, and a transverse section of it is very like unto ebony both in smoothness and in color. This exterior cortex, however, is not skin (*cutis*), but cuticle (*cuticula*); but in the dorsal region it is smooth. From the nape to the caudal fin the surface is uneven with nothing but circular wrinkles, but the sides are exceedingly rough, especially about the head, and bristling with many cup-shaped prominences like stemless mushrooms (*pezicas*). This cuticle which surrounds the whole body like a crust is frequently an inch in thickness; and it is composed of nothing but tubules, in the same way as we observe in the Spanish cane or *Mambu* of the Indians and Chinese (*ac in arundine videmus Hispanicove Mambu Indorum et Sinensium*). The structure of these tubules is perpendicular to the skin. Longitudinally they can not be torn or separated from one another. The tubules are implanted in the lower part of the skin; they are roundish, convex, bulbous, and hence pieces of the skin that are torn off from the cuticle are full of tubercles like Spanish bark, and the underlying cutis is excavated with a great many very small holes, like a thimble (*netricum digitale*), which were before the receptacles of the bulbous tubules of the cuticle. Now, these tubules rest upon one another very closely; they are tenacious, wet, and tumid, and they do not appear when the cuticle is cut horizontally, but the surface is smooth, as the hoofs of certain animals when they are cut. But as soon as it is hung up in pieces and exposed to the sun and becomes dry, it has perpendicular fissures and can be broken like bark, and then this tubulous structure comes clearly to view. Through these tubes a thin, serous mucus is exuded, in larger quantities on the sides and about the head, and in smaller quantities on the back. When the animal has lain for some hours upon the dry shore, the back becomes dry, but the head and sides are always wet.

Now, this thick cuticle seems given to the animal for two purposes principally: (1) That, inasmuch as the animal is compelled, for the sake of getting a living, to live continously in rough and rugged places, and in the winter among the ice, it may not rub off the skin, or that it may not be beaten by the heavy waves and bruised with the stones, and when pursued it is protected by this coat of mail; (2) that the natural heat may not be dissipated in the summer by too profuse perspiration (*nimium transpirando*), or completely counteracted by the cold of winter. And that would be natural, for it has to live, not in the depths of the sea as other animals and fishes, but it is always compelled in feeding to expose half of its body to the cold.

I have observed in the case of many that were cast up dead upon the shore of the sea, that the cuticle had been broken off on one side or the other, and that that had been the cause of their death; and this happens principally in the winter time, from the ice.

And I observed many times in animals that had been captured and drawn on shore with a hook, that great pieces of cuticle had been pulled off in consequence of the violent thrashing of its body and tail and its resisting with its front feet, and that the broken piece of cuticle that covered the arms and caudal fin was like a hoof; all this goes to make my opinion stronger. Cuticle of exactly the same sort covers the whale (*balaena*), although no mention is made of it by the authorities; and almost the whole of the cuticle was rubbed off from a whale that was washed up dead upon our island on the 1st day of August, for during several days it had been tossed about by the waves, this way and that, and bruised upon the rocks before it came to our shore.

While this cuticle is wet it is tawny black, like the skin of a smoked ham, but when it is dry it is wholly black. In certain animals it is marked with rather large white spots and zones, and this color penetrates clear to the cutis. This cuticle about the head, eyes, ears, breasts, and under the arms, where it is rough, is thickly infested by insects, and it frequently happens that they perforate the cuticle and wound even the cutis itself. When this happens, large, thick, warty prominences arise from the lymph of the cutis, or from the broken glands that preserve the oil, as it were, in the little cells, in the same manner as in whales, and oftentimes make the above-mentioned places foul.

Under the cuticle lies the cutis surrounding the whole body. This is 2 lines thick, soft, white, very firm in strength and structure just like that of the whale, and it can be put to the same uses.

In comparison with the huge mass of the rest of its body the head is small, short, and closely connected with the body; in figure it is a square oblong, widening from the top toward the lower jaw. The top itself is flat and covered with a black cuticle, exceedingly scraggly and a third part thinner than the rest of the cuticle and more easily torn off. The head slopes from the occiput to the nares and slopes again from the nares to the lips. The end of the snout is 8 inches high and grows rapidly thicker from the nose to the occiput.

The opening of the mouth (*rictus oris*) is not underneath (*supinus*), but in a line with the sides; but the exterior upper lip is so large, broad, and oblique to the angle of the mouth, and lengthened out so much above the inferior mandible, that to one who looks at the head alone the opening seems to be located underneath.

The opening of the month itself is not very large in proportion to the animal, nor is it necessary that it should be, as it lives on seaweed.

The lips, both the upper and the lower, are double and divided into external and internal lips.

The external upper lip, finishing the end of the snout obliquely, is like a half circle; it is flat, tumid, thick, 14 inches broad, 10 inches high, in color a glossy white, and overgrown with a great many little hills or tubercles, from the center of each one of which grows a white, translucent bristle 4 or 5 inches long.

The internal upper lip is 5 inches long and 2½ inches wide. It is everywhere detached from the external lip, and fastened to it only at the base; it overhangs the palate, and it looks like a calf's tongue, all villous and rough like a brush. It closes the mouth firmly above; it is movable, and by its own motion serves to tear off the seaweed and bring it into its mouth; for it feeds in the same way as horses and cattle, by protruding its lips and bending them outward.

The lower lip is likewise double; the external lip is black, and smooth, and without bristles; it is roughly heart-shaped and like a chin, if we may so call it; it is 7 inches wide and 6.8 inches high.

The internal lower lip is separated likewise from the external; it is villous and is not visible when the mouth is closed, because the external lip reaches out and covers it; and being set opposite the internal upper lip it closes the mouth firmly.

When the lower mandible is applied to the upper, the space which intervenes when both are closed is filled up with a dense array of very thick white bristles 1½ inches long. These bristles prevent anything from falling out of the mouth while the animal masticates, or from being washed out with water which flows into the mouth and is driven out again through the opening when the mouth is closed.

The bristles are as thick as a dove's quill; they are white, hollow inside, bulbous below, and, even without the aid of a microscope, they show clearly the structure of the human hair.

If the animal lies prone upon its belly, the end of its snout on a line perpendicular from the nares to the lips is 8 inches high and is rounded in front, like a ball, from the nose to the ends of the lips and also to the lateral regions of the upper jaw. It grows thicker and increases rapidly in circumference. The external lips are very prominent, thick and swollen, and perforated with a great many large pores, like a cat's, from each one of which grows a strong white bristle; these bristles are perceptibly stouter the nearer they are to the opening of the mouth itself. Of the bristles those were especially noticeable for thickness which grow between the lips of either jaw. They take the place of teeth in pulling off the seaweed and prevent anything from falling out of the mouth while the animal masticates. The inferior maxilla is shorter than the superior; it alone is movable, but the lips of both maxillae move, as do the lips of cattle. With these the submarine plants which they tear off from the rocks with their arms are so cut off from the hard, uneatable roots and stems that they seem to be cut off with the edge of a dull knife. When the tide comes in these roots and stems are washed ashore, and lying there in great heaps on the seashore they betray to the visitor the present quarters of these guests, inasmuch as the stems of sea plants are tougher and thicker than those of land plants, the lips are made much stronger and harder than are the lips of any of the land animals; therefore the lips are also inedible, and can not be softened by boiling or in any other way. The internal structure of the lips is so arranged that when cut they are like a checkerboard, consisting of very small squares; there are countless very small, thick, red, rhomboid or trapezoid squares, with which others that are white, tendinous, full of cells like network and containing liquid oil, are interspersed in equal numbers. These lips when boiled in water very easily yield a great amount of oil, and when this oil is tried out the white cells appear like so much tendinous network. The purpose of this structure seems to me to be a threefold one: (1) That the strength and density of the lips may be increased, and that they may not be so easily exposed to any danger from without; (2) that the heavy lips may be more easily raised and moved, inasmuch as the origin and insertion of the muscles (*caput et caudae horum musculorum*) are so disposed that the origin of the muscles is set obliquely to the opening of the mouth, and the insertion of the muscles obliquely to the top of the head; so that with their beginnings and ends the lips make, as it were, a wreath of muscles; (3) that by means of this structure the lips may be moved with a sort of spiral motion, and that, since the head on account of the continuous thick crust can be moved only with difficulty, it may not be necessary for them to move the whole body as often as they wish to pull off the tenacious seaweed.

They masticate differently from all other animals; not with teeth, which they lack altogether, but with two strong white bones, or solid tooth masses, one of which is set in the palate and the other is fastened in the inferior maxilla, and corresponds to the first.

The insertion itself, or connection, is entirely anomalous, and would be expressed by no known name; *gomphosis* we can not call it, because the bones are not fastened in the maxillae, but each is held by many papillae and pores, pores and papillae alternating, in the palate and in the inferior mandible. Besides, in front it is inserted into the papillary membrane of the internal upper lip, and at the sides in the grooved edge of the bone, and at the back, with a double process, into the palate and inferior maxilla, and is in this way made firm.

These molar bones are perforated below with many little holes, like a thimble (*netricum digitale*), or like a sponge, in which the arteries and nerves are inserted in the same way as in the teeth of other animals. Above they are smooth and excavated with many winding, wavy canals, and between them are eminences which in mastication fit into the canals of the corresponding bone so perfectly that the seaweed (*fuci*) is ground and mashed between them as between a fuller's beams or between millstones. I have had a drawing made of these bones, which will explain more clearly what is less intelligible from the description.

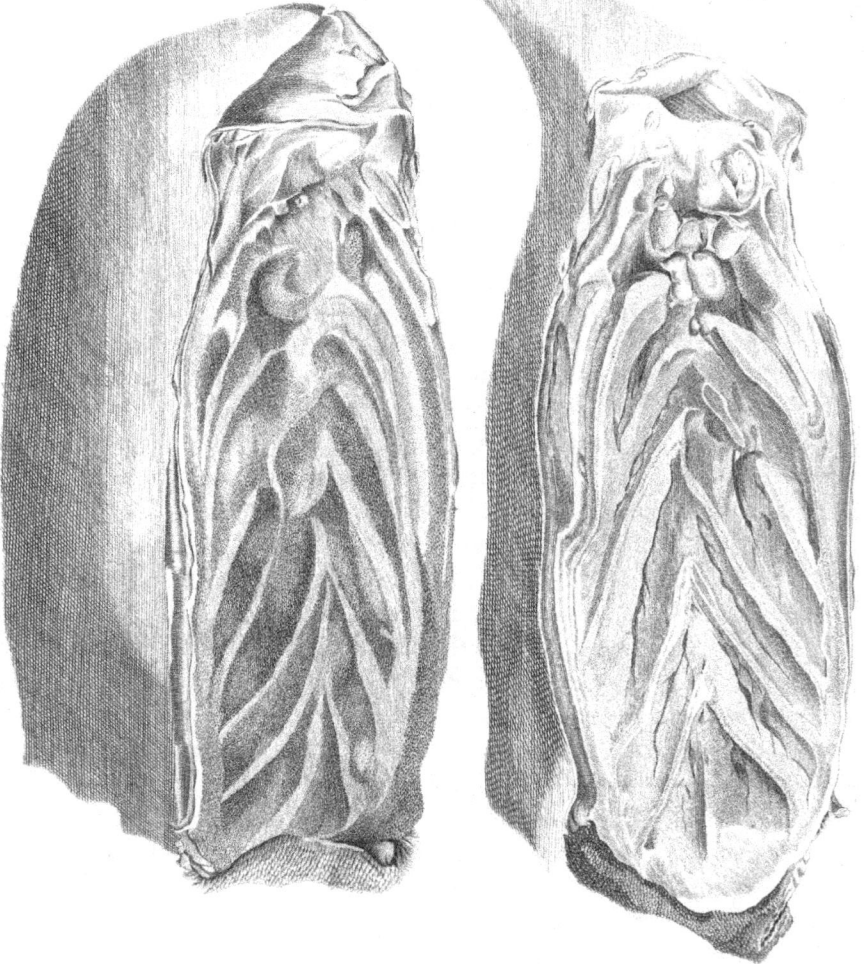

comm. Nov. Ac. Sc. Petr.Tom.II Tab.XIV

The nose is situated in the farthest tip of the head, as in the horse; there are two nostrils, and a thick cartilaginous column 1½ inches wide between them. The nostrils themselves are 2 inches long and just as wide in diameter. They are flat, and stretch back with many curves or labyrinths. Inside, the nostrils are very wide, wrinkled, and covered over with a nervous membrane, which is perforated with many black pores. From each pore grows a bristle as thick as cobbler's waxed-end, a half inch long; they are easy to pull out, and they take the place of *vibrissae* in other animals.

The eyes are situated exactly half way between the end of the snout and the ears in a line parallel with the top of the nostrils, or just a very little higher. They are very small in proportion to so huge a body, being no larger than a sheep's eyes. They are not provided with shutters, or lids, or any other external apparatus, but protrude from the skin through a round opening, scarcely a half inch in diameter. The iris of the eye is black, the ball livid; the canthi of the eye are not seen except when the skin is cut away around the opening of the eye. At the inner canthus of the eye there is a cartilaginous crest (precisely like that of the sea otter), which, when necessity arises, covers over the whole eye and takes the place of a nictitating membrane adapted to warding off and removing any injury that might chance to fall while the animal feeds. This cartilaginous crest in the back part constitutes one wall of the lachrymal sac, with which it is joined by a common nervous membrane. When the lachrymal sac is cut a great amount of sticky mucus is found in its cavity. The sac itself would easily hold a chestnut, and inside it is enveloped in a glandular membrane.

The ears outside open only with a small hole, like the seal's. There is not the slightest trace of an external ear, and the holes can be seen only by examining very closely; for the opening of the ears can not be distinguished from the rest of the pores, and would scarcely admit the quill of a chicken's feather. The internal canal of the ears is smooth and covered with a highly polished black skin, and when the muscles of the occiput are separated from it, as they may easily be, it betrays itself by its own color and can be seen.

The tongue is 12 inches long and 2½ inches wide; and is like that of an ox. It is pointed at the end and the surface is rough with short papillae like a file. It is so deeply hidden away in the fauces that to many the animal has seemed to be without a tongue; for drawn as far forward as it may be by the hand, it still can not be made to reach the *froenum*, but will fall short of it by 1½ inches. If it were longer, as in other animals, it would be in the way in mastication.

The head, like the neck, is ill defined, and joins the body in such a way that a line of distinction is nowhere visible, as is the case with all fishes; but what obscurely suggests a neck is shorter by one-half than the head itself, and is cylindrical and more slender than the occiput in circumference. Notwithstanding, it is not only constructed with movable vertebrae, but has its independent action, a motion observed in the living animal only when it feeds; for it bends its head in the same way as cattle on dry land, but the thick and shapeless cuticle makes the quiet or dead animal look as though it were provided with an immovable neck, for no trace of vertebrae is to be seen at all.

From the shoulders toward the umbilical region it grows rapidly wider, and from there on to the anus it again grows rapidly slender; the sides are roundish and paunched like a belly which is swollen with a great mass of intestines, and elastic and puffed up like an inflated skin, and diminishes in size from the umbilical region toward the anus, and again from the mammae toward the neck.

When the animals are fat, as they are in spring and summer, the back is slightly convex; but in winter, when they are thin, the back is flat and excavated at the spine with a hollow on either side, and at such times all the vertebrae with their spinous processes can be seen.

The ribs rise on both sides in an arch to the back, and where they are joined to the vertebrae of the back by *amphiarthrosis*, as they are in a man, they extend downward like a bow, and in the place where they are joined on both sides to the vertebrae they make a double hollow on the back.

At the twenty-sixth vertebra the tail begins, and continues with thirty-five vertebrae. The tail grows perceptibly thinner toward the fin. It is not so much flat as rather somewhat quadrangular, for all the vertebrae of the tail have two epiphyses [zygapophyses] and four processes. Of these the lateral processes are broad, flat, and blunt at the point. The spinous process on the dorsal side or spine (*processus superior in dorso seu spina*) is sharpened; the lower one is a broad, flat bone, like unto a Greek lambda. This is joined by a cord to the main body of the tail and is fastened to it with very strong ligaments and tendons. As a result of this quadruple position the muscles of the tail fill these cavities of the vertebrae and the angles between the processes, and so the tail itself gets the form of a square oblong with obtuse angles.

For the rest the tail is thick, very powerful, and ends in a very hard, stiff, black fin, which is not divided into rays, but solid, and is in substance like prepared whale-bone, and consists of nothing but layers, one upon the other, as if one solid piece. This fin is frayed out for a distance of 9 inches from the extremity, and is something like the fins of fishes that are spined with a ruder sort of spines. The fin itself that ends the tail is 78 inches wide or long, 7.3 inches high, and 1.5 inches thick, and is inserted in the muscles of the tail as if by *gomphosis*, or a triangular canal.*

The fin of the tail is somewhat forked, and both cornua, differently from the tail fins of larger sea fishes, as the shark and the like, are of the same magnitude. In this respect it agrees with the whale. And so the caudal fin is parallel with the sides, as is the case of the phocaena and balaena, and not with the back, as is the case with most fishes. With a gentle sidewise motion of its tail it swims gently forward; with an up-and-down motion of the tail it drives itself violently forward and struggles to escape from the hands of enemies who are trying to draw it in.

The strangest feature of all, in which this animal differs from all other animals both of land and sea and from amphibia, is its arms, or, if you please, its front feet; for two arms, 26.5 inches long, consisting of two articulations, are joined immediately to the shoulders at the neck. The end of the humerus is joined to the scapula by *arthrodia*.

The ulna and radius are like a man's; the ulna and radius terminate bluntly with tarsus and metatarsus. There are no traces of fingers, nor are there any of nails or hoofs; but the tarsus and metatarsus are covered with solid fat, many tendons and ligaments, cutis and cuticle, as an amputated human limb is covered with skin. But both the cutis, and especially the cuticle, are much thicker, harder, and drier there, and so the ends of the arms are something like claws, or rather like a horse's hoof; but a horse's hoof is sharper and more pointed, and so

---

* There is an evident omission here, as these measurements would give the animal an absurdly narrow tail, whereas we know from the references to the power of the animal, as well as from the figures that have been preserved, that the flukes were broad and powerful. The vertebræ and their muscles lie in the fibrous mass of the flukes as if driven in. — ED. [1899 note]

better suited to digging. On the back (*supine*) these claws are smooth and convex, but underneath they are flat and hollowed out in a way, and rough with countless very closely set bristles, half an inch long and hard like a brush.

I have seen in one animal these claws divided into two parts, like an ox's hoof. The division, however, was no more than marked, and that only in the cuticle; this happened more by mere chance than by the will of nature, and was the more easy and the more possible as the cuticle that covered the claws was disposed on account of its dryness to crack.

Now, this Platonic man, as the eminent John Ray was pleased in jest to call him, performs with these arms various offices: with these he swims, as with branchial fins; with these he walks on the shallows of the shore, as with feet; with these he braces and supports himself on the slippery rocks; with these he digs out and tears off the algae and seagrasses from the rocks, as a horse would do with its front feet; with these he fights, and when taken with a hook and dragged from the water upon dry land he resists so vehemently that the cuticle surrounding these arms is often torn and pulled off in pieces; and finally with these the female when smitten with the sting of passion, swimming prone upon her back, embraces her covering lover and holds him and permits herself in turn to be embraced.

The two breasts are different from those of most other animals, but in place and form are exactly as in man; they are situated one under each arm; and one breast is a foot and a half in diameter, convex, rough with many spiral wrinkles, full of glands, very hard — harder than a cow's — and without any intermingling fat. But the adipose tissue that surrounds the whole body rests upon them only with the same thickness as everywhere else, but the cuticle is thinner there and softer, and more wrinkled, and the papillae are likewise surrounded with a black cuticle with circular wrinkles, but soft. Under the arm itself, or axilla, the breast hangs, and when the animal is in milk the nipple is 4 inches long and 1½ inches in diameter; in those, however, which have gone dry, or have not yet given birth, it is so short and contracted that it seems nothing more than a chance wart, for the breast is not swollen.

The milk is very rich and sweet, and in consistency is very much like sheep's milk, and very often it was my wont to get the milk in large quantities from dead ones in the same way as from cows. The nipple is very much wrinkled and a little higher than the rest of the breast. When the glands are cut they give out milk which is like that which I collected by squeezing the papillae. Ten or twelve lacteal ducts open into each papilla. The breasts when boiled are a little harder than beef, and give out the odor of game, but mild.

They come together after the human fashion, the male above and the female below. The penis of the male is 32 inches long, and with its sheath is bound firmly in front to the abdomen, and reaches clear to the navel — in a word, it is very coarse and obscene to look upon, very much like that of a horse, and ends with the same sort of a gland, only larger.

The female pudenda lie 8 inches above the anus. The opening of the vulva is almost a triangle, and wider above, where the clitoris lies, and narrower toward the anus. The opening itself would without difficulty admit five fingers together. The clitoris is about 1½ inches long. It is cartilaginous and surrounded with a very strong, smooth skin, and is uneven, with many short wrinkles that fold together. The skin is variegated with yellow and white, and so is the vulva. The labia vulvae are very rigid and hard. The urethra empties into the vulva about 5 inches from the opening of the vulva. Below this is stretched a strong, crescent-shaped membrane, partly muscular and partly tendinous, which separates the vulva from the *vagina uteri*, properly so called, with a sort of vestibule, and makes a kind of hymen. But the aperture between the cornua of this membrane is so large that the penis of the male can without any difficulty enter the vagina. The vagina itself is 9½ inches long and covered with a very strong, fibrous membrane, which is ribbed longitudinally and hollowed out upon its surface with many furrows; between these furrows are seen a great many glands not larger than a pin's head, which secrete the mucus with which the vagina is covered all over. Next appears the uterus itself, spherical in shape, in size as large as the head of a cat. When I cut it open it was covered with mucus in the same way as the vagina, and wrinkled with a great number of folds half an inch wide. The substance of the vagina was so hard that I could scarcely cut it with a knife. The ligaments of the uterus and of the fallopian tubes had precisely the same structure as those of a horse.

The anus is situated 8½ inches below the pudenda. It is closed by a sphincter that is not very tightly contracted. In diameter it is 4 inches wide. The sphincter is white; the inside coating of the rectal intestine is smooth, slippery, olive-gray, just as in horses, where it is sometimes black, sometimes white spotted.

Description of the Internal Parts

I opened the heads of four animals, and with the greatest painstaking I searched for the stones, incorrectly so called, of the manatee. But so far was I from being able to find anything in the least like a stone or bone that from this I decided that either those bones were not found in all of them, or were, found only in certain climates, or, what seemed more probable, that Schröder and others who describe these bones as having the form of a ball, had, like too superficial and untrustworthy compilers, given it this round form after the analogy of the bezoar stone, and that they had never with their eyes seen stones or bones of the manatee as they described; and so we should rather understand that they meant the masticatory bones, or those white tooth masses to be found in the palate and inferior maxilla; and this was the more likely, as the description given by the eminent Samuel von Dale in his Pharmacologia coincides with my own; and his description also corresponds to these masticatory bones. For he gives, perhaps from autopsy (*ex αυτοψια*), because he did not understand the mechanism of these bones, the following description: "The stone of the manatee is a white crustaceous bone similar to ivory, taken from the head, and it is of various forms," by which he no doubt meant to indicate the openings and meanderings of various forms to be seen upon the surface of both bones.*

The cranium is very solid; it has but little cerebrum, and the cerebrum is not separated from the cerebellum by any bony plate. Of the rest I could observe nothing striking.

The oesophagus or gullet is very capacious. Inside it is surrounded with a very tough, white, fibrous membrane, and with many perpendicular wrinkles and folds it goes to the stomach, and there, before it ends, it concludes with a large number of little triangular appendices

---

* These bones are undoubtedly the ear bones, and that Steller failed to find them is due to the fact that he looked for them *inside* the cranial cavity. The ear bones of Rytina are not unlike those of the existing Manatee. — ED. [1899 note]

one line long, which turn back upward toward the oesophagus. The use of these is, I think, that they may hinder the reflux of the food back into the gullet, and at first sight they refute the preposterous opinion that has been held in regard to the animal's being a ruminant.

The oesophagus is inserted into the stomach nearly at the middle, as in the horse and the hare.

The stomach is of stupendous size, 6 feet long, 5 feet wide, and so stuffed with food and seaweed that four strong men with a rope attached to it could with great effort scarcely move it from its place and drag it out.

The coats of the stomach could not by any means be separated; together they were 3 lines thick. A very strange fat omentum 2 lines thick surrounds the stomach. In the upper part it adheres firmly at the middle to the membranous coat of the stomach; for the rest, it is detached and seems more to warm the stomach with its own heat than to hold it in place. The inner coat of the stomach is white, smooth, and not wrinkled nor villous. But what was most peculiar, and perhaps incredible to many, is that I found contained in the stomach, and not far from the entrance of the oesophagus into the stomach, an oval gland as large as a man's head, and grown fast to it something like a large aneurism between the muscular and fibrous (*nervosa*) coat; this gland opened through the villous coat with many pores and openings and exuded into the cavity of the stomach a great quantity of whitish liquid, in consistency and color like pancreatic juice. I had as a witness of this curious phenomenon the assistant surgeon, Bettge. What the character of this juice was I discovered by a double chance experiment; when I inserted a silver tube through the pores of the inner coat, in order to discover by blowing into them the excretory ducts, the tube came out black, as is wont to happen when silver touches sulphurous acid. I observed the same thing when I ordered Archippus Konovalow, the helper of the assistant surgeon, to take out the contents of the stomach with his hands, and when this was done a silver ring that he had upon his finger was stained with the same color.

The inner coat of the stomach was perforated by white worms half a foot long, with which the whole stomach, pylorus and duodenum, swarmed; and the worms had penetrated clear into the cavity of the glands. The gland when cut poured out a great quantity of juice. After that I could not examine any more stomachs, because I lacked

the necessary assistance; and with the few men I had I could not, if I
found an animal lying anywhere, turn it over upon its back; and therefore I am in doubt whether this gland is a constant thing or rather the
result of some disease.

The pylorus was so large and tumid that at first sight I took it for a
second stomach and was anxious to find the two others, too, because I
thought the animal was a ruminant. But when I cut into the pylorus I
was otherwise informed, and from its being like the stomach I saw that
it was the pylorus. But to my misfortune it happened that the pancreas
along with the duct into the duodenum and the ductus choledochus
were cut, for the simple reason that the stomach could not be taken out
whole with the liver on account of its great size, and besides, my assis-
tants, who had been hired for just one' hour with tobacco, which took
the place of money, became tired of the work. Yet I recognized that
the pancreas was divided into two lobes and composed of many flat,
rather large glands, and that it was, for so large an animal, compara-
tively small; for it did not extend in length beyond 4 inches.

There are more intestines in this animal than in any other, except,
perhaps, the whale alone, which hitherto I have not been in a position
to inspect. The abdominal cavity was so full that the abdomen was tumid and swollen like an inflated skin. Hence, when the common cov-
erings and muscles of the abdomen were removed and the peritoneum
received ever so slight a wound, the wind came out with such a whistle
and hum as it is wont to come from an aeolipile. For the same reason
the whole abdomen is covered with a very strong double, membranous, fibrous peritoneum for holding in the intestines. The peritoneum reaches from the os pubis to the sternum, and is attached on
both sides to the false ribs, from each one of which strong tendons,
spreading out in many rectilinear branches, run from both sides to the
linea alba; and when the muscles of the abdomen on the surface of the
peritoneum are removed the tendons meeting each other and cross-
ing each other make the surface of the peritoneum tessellated like a
checkerboard, and present a pleasing spectacle to the eye. Other like
tendons grow from the inner side of the ribs and are seen to inter-
twine (*impexi*) tightly with the peritoneum on the inside, increasing its
firmness as with horizontal processes. Both membranes run into a single one in the middle about the linea alba, but toward the sides they
are double.

When the peritoneum is cut the intestines gush out violently, and without any outside assistance they move from their original place, because they are found always so tightly stuffed that from oesophagus to anus they make a solid pack without any open space. The thin intestines are smooth, rolled up in a great amount of fat; they are round and 6 inches broad in diameter. If only a very slight aperture should be made with the point of a knife, the liquid excrement (a ridiculous thing to behold) would squirt out violently like blood from a ruptured vein; and not infrequently the face of the spectator would be drenched by this springing fountain whenever some one opened a canal upon his neighbor opposite, for a joke.

The coecum was very large, as was also the colon, and by a ligament that extended lengthwise on either side was divided into many little cells. But the valve of the colon I could not find, search as I might. To be brief, the intestines were different from a horse's in size and capacity alone, but not in structure. And so the final product of this workshop is so like the excrement of horses, in shape, size, smell, and color, and all other attributes, that it would deceive the most expert stable boy. And I will not deny that on the first days after our arrival on the island I was ignominiously deceived; I considered it no slight marvel, but I did not make the boast to have found what the boys did in the beans (*faba; fabula* (?)),when I found the stuff frozen together and so inexplicable (*cimmelium*). Now, I, not knowing from whence it came, argued from utterly false premises to an absolutely true conclusion that America lay opposite this island and not far away (for up to that time the continent had not been seen on account of the autumnal fog). But since horses are not kept in Kamchatka, but are kept in parts of America, the fact that the dung was brought over there whole and not dissolved, was an unquestionable proof of the proximity of land.

The whole intestinal tract, from gullet to anus, when this Augean stable was thoroughly cleansed, measured fully 5,968 inches, and so the intestines are twenty and a half times as long as the whole living animal.

The mesentery is exceedingly thick and half covered with a mass of little glands, varying in size from that of the acorn to that of the walnut. The lacteal, as well as the lymphatic vessels, I could not observe because of the opacity of the very fat, thick mesentery, although

I searched while the intestines were still warm, for the veins are only obscurely and darkly transparent, inasmuch as they are as thick as one's finger.

A very strong, double membrane constitutes the pleura. Inside this, one continuous muscle an inch thick is interposed and covers both sides.

The urinary bladder, 2 lines thick, was very strong, but not larger than a man's head, and smaller than the bladder of an ox.

The trachea is composed of long, cartilaginous circles or semicircles, but has an entirely anomalous structure. One continuous piece of cartilage is twisted into a spiral and covered with a strong continuous membrane, both inside and outside. But the spirals of the trachea are not everywhere equal in breadth, but in some places the edge of the upper circle is hollowed out to receive the opposite eminence of the lower circle, and so makes it crooked. And so, by the help of this double membrane that encircles the trachea, the spirals are kept from being dislocated, either inside or outside. Through this mutual intertwining the rings are prevented from being loosened laterally. By this spiral structure the trachea is separated into branches below the glottis and reaches to the bronchi, and is seen to be such in the very substance of the lungs; it is so constructed for no other reason, perhaps, than that by the continuity of these spirals the huge mass of lungs may be more easily lifted up in breathing; for neither muscles nor anything else give so much help to the motion of lungs, which are situated in the back.

The glottis is like that of an ox, but is closed by the epiglottis much more closely and firmly than is the case in the land quadrupeds, so the epiglottis is in proportion much thicker. The diameter of the trachea below the glottis is 4.2 inches.

The thyroid gland is very large, and when cut it poured out a large quantity of liquid of double consistency and color: that which came from the larger exterior glands when cut was of the color of milk, but thicker than sheep's milk, and sweet to the taste; that which came from the middle portion of the gland or receptacle for the gland was contained in a membranous sac of its own; it was glutinous and had the consistency of meal poultice; it was somewhat sweet, with a very slight taste of bitter, and was yellowish-white in color. It occurred to me only in the last animal that I opened to make a closer inspection of this gland. I am very sorry that I did not think of it sooner, and take the pains to have the trachea, with the gullet, heart, and the rest of the viscera taken out entire. But it was not possible without the help of many men to do so with an animal so huge. If I had been in a position to do that, I should have observed whether or not it unloaded this liquid through some tube into a duct of its own, or into the stomach, as Vercellonius thought, or somewhere else. I saw the duct only after it was cut, but whither it led I neither saw nor do I wish to conjecture.

As to the heart it differs in many respects from the heart of all other animals: (1) In regard to situation, the apex of the heart stands in a line oblique to the sternum, the base in a line oblique to the back. (2) As to connection, the heart does not rest against the mediastinum, but is detached on every side and has no mediastinum at all. (3) It has a pericardium (but this does not envelope the heart closely) and a sac; but it forms rather a species of cavity in the thorax and lines the thorax. Toward the back and the base of the heart the pericardium is nearer to the heart than it is anywhere else. When the animal is feeding, the heart itself, with the pericardium, hangs not quite perpendicularly but somewhat obliquely from back to sternum; and so there the pericardium takes the place of a mediastinum. Lower down toward the abdomen the pericardium is fastened to the inner wall of the diaphragm, and with it constitutes one wall; and so it rests against the pleura at the sides. (4) As to size, when placed in a scale it weighed 34¾ pounds, and was from base to apices 2 feet 2 inches long, and from the extremity of one auricle to the other 2½ feet broad; and so it was broader than it was long. (5) As to form, it was broad and thick, rather than long, and what was the greatest peculiarity of all it ended, not like a top in one apex but, in accordance with the number of ventricles, in two apices. Now, this slit in the apex extends to one-third the length of the heart, and from there on the two apices coalesce in one and form the septum of the heart, dividing the ventricles. The left apex is just a little longer than the right and thicker in circumference. The ventricles of the heart are extended farther below the septum, each into its own apex. The chordae tendineae and the columnae carniae (*cordis trabes*) or *sulci* (furrows) exceed the equipment of the human heart, not only in size and strength but also in number. The valves are the same in the pulmonary vein, the vena cava, the aorta, and the pulmonary artery, as in a man. The base of the heart is surrounded with a great quantity of thick fat that is placed around it like packing, distributed everywhere to the thickness of half an inch. Below this the large coronary veins of the heart are seen, covered inside with little valves which I have never observed anywhere else before in any other animal. With great care I searched for the foramen ovale and for the ductus arteriosus Botalli, but in vain. When I cut through the cavity of the pericardium I found it half full of liquid, so that even by this quantity alone I was led to believe that this liquid was unnatural (*praeter naturalem*), and that at the end it had been collected into this cavity, from whatsoever source it may have been secreted, in consequence of the slow and distressing death of the animal.

The lungs are two very long, white lobes that extend to the middle of the abdomen, one on either side along the dorsal spine. They are, however, detached, and not fastened anywhere, in which respect they differ from the lungs of birds, although they agree with them in respect to their position in the back. Either lobe is covered outside with a very strong membrane, and so if one should think only of the external structure and color of the lungs one would scarcely consider them to be lungs at all.

The liver consists of two very large lobes and a third of quite peculiar form; the third is almost square and looks like a blacksmith's anvil. It is situated half way between the two larger lobes, and is raised above them and lies immediately under the sternum. Outside, the liver is covered with a very strong fibrous membrane, so that it suggests anything but a liver. Through this membrane, in the gibbous part, the branches of the coeliac vessels (*venae celiacae*) excessively tumid, shine through like a tree, blue in color. When this membrane was cut the substance of the liver appeared, in color a tawny yellow, like that of an ox, but externally soft and most delicate in structure, so that at the touch it dissolved as if putrid under my hand.

The animal has no gall bladder. But the ductus choledochus, like that of a horse, would easily admit five fingers together; and so it was very capacious; it was half a line thick and very strong, whitish outside and yellow inside, and, opening into the duodenum, it coalesces along with the pancreatic duct into one canal.

The kidneys are hidden away in a cavity of the lumbar region on either side of the dorsal spine. They are 32 inches long and 18 inches wide; they have the ordinary form of kidneys and are included in a very strong membrane; when this was removed there appeared a great number of renules of the same form, as in the seal and the sea otter, but in size they were much larger than these. They were 2 inches long and 1½ inches wide on the surface, and they were pyramidal in form toward the interior. Each one of these lobules (*renunculi*) is provided with an urethra, papillae, and artery of its own. The urethras form six larger principal branches, and at last carry down the urine through one canal to the urinary bladder. But the pelvis ia like an elephant's.

I overlooked the suprarenal capsules (*capsulae atribilariae*), and also the spleen, and likewise the internal organs of generation, and many other things which occurred to me in order only when I had no longer time nor opportunity for making full observations.

Brief Description of the Bones

As to the bones of the manatee, the bones of the head in respect to strength and firmness are like those of a horse, but in respect to size and thickness they surpass the bones of all animals of the land.

The bones of the head taken together are not larger than a horse's head, nor are they very different in respect to form and articulation.

The cranium is anteriorly entire, without any suture, extending toward the nasal bones* in two hard processes, and joining the nasal and maxillary bones by an arthrodia, while the nasals join the maxillaries by ginglimus. The nasal bones meet in a rough suture. The temporal bone joins the cranium by suture, but the occipital by coalescence, being very hard and almost like rock. The inferior maxillary in adults consists of one bone, in calves of two.

The head from the nares to the occiput is 27 inches long, and at the occiput 13½ inches wide.†

There are sixty vertebrae in all: six in the neck, nineteen in the back, and thirty-five in the tail.

There are five pairs of true ribs and twelve of false.

The body of the vertebrae of the neck is narrow, in general structure like the vertebrae of the horse's neck. How much they differ in

---

* Really the frontals. — ED. [1899 note]
† Given in the previous table as 10½. — ED. [1899 note]

certain special features I will not indicate, as I have no books nor a horse's skeleton, nor should I trust my memory or imagination.

The spines of the dorsal vertebrae are sharp and broad, and in lean animals, as there is no thick cuticle or thick adipose tissue in the way, they are perfectly visible.

The vertebrae of the back in the region of the stomach and liver are ridged on the inside, but all the rest are rounded and lack this sharpened prominence.

The vertebrae of the tail have each four processes; the lateral processes are long and broad; the superior process is like the lateral process in width but is shorter; and the inferior processes (chevrons) are single bones like the Greek lambda in shape, and are fastened to the body of the vertebrae by a cord and held firmly with very strong ligaments. All the vertebrae are joined together longitudinally by a great number of very strong, broad tendons, and are everywhere so covered up that because of them the bones can not be seen.

The five pairs of true ribs are joined to the sternum with cartilage. Both the true and the false ribs are all solid and very heavy and thick.

The sternum in the upper portion where the ribs are fastened on is cartilaginous; in the lower portion toward the notch of the heart (*scrobiculum cordis*) it is bony to a distance of a foot and a half.

In place of the innominate bone of the hip there are two bones, one on each side in size and form like the ulna of the human skeleton, and joined with very strong ligaments to the thirty-fifth vertebra on one side and to the os pubis on the other. It has no clavicles.

The arms consist of two bones, tarsus and metatarsus.

Description of Its Habits and Nature

I should have abstained from an extended description of this animal if I had not observed that there are in existence some brief and imperfect histories of the manatee, swarming with fables and false theories after the manner of the last century and the century before, in which the writers of natural history saw only through a lattice what they might have seen with their eyes; when investigating the unknown habits of animals, their character, and a thousand other things that have nothing to do with their subject, they only involved the best known facts in more than Cimmerian darkness.

Therefore I have endeavored to give a clear and succinct idea of its external form and that of the structure of its internal parts by stating its agreement and disagreement with others, next by explaining the mechanism and nature of the animal, and after that the use of its parts for food, medicine, and other things, and finally to add in perfect truth what I observed with my own eyes in regard to the movements, nature, and habits of the living animal.

Various things combined to cause me many disappointments. The weather at the time when the animals were captured was almost constantly rainy and cold; my observations had to be made in the daytime; then there were the tides of the sea; and the droves of blue foxes (*isatides*) would spoil everything with their teeth and steal from under my very hands; they carried away my maps, book, and ink when I was studying the animal and worried me when I was writing; the great size of the animal itself and the bulk of its parts were also a hindrance, as I had to be both observer and workman, as all the rest were anxious about the construction of a ship and our liberation from the island. At my own expense I could hire them for barely an hour at evening time for some of the simpler assistance, and in their ignorance and dislike for the work they would tear everything to pieces, and acted according to their own inclinations; so the injury they wrought and the loss they caused ought to be commended in that they did not desert me entirely. Not a single gut could I get out entire, nor unfold if I had got it out, so as to do anything worth while; so that for all the pleasure I got from certain observations I had twice as much trouble and annoyance in consequence of those useful things which I had to leave alone. So I beg of my kind readers, when they have finished reading this feeble description, that they will judge it by my will and my zeal rather than by the circumstances.

I had prepared a skeleton of a manatee calf, and I had taken the cutis with the cuticle separated from it and stuffed it with grass to bring it home with me; but when I saw that on account of the small size of our craft this was impossible I wanted to bring with me at least the spoils (skin), but even this wish was vain. I intended to do the same with the sea lion, the sea bear and the sea otter, but I was reckoning without my host, for in Kamchatka there is no hope of getting everything.

But let me cease from narrating my complaints and my hindrances. The manatee is not the sea cow of Aristotle, for it never comes upon dry land to feed. And it is of little consequence whether it is the same or not, for it is not this animal that he described; indeed, he never saw it and never heard anything about it to tell. In the second place, I remark that Lopez Francisco Hernandes themselves saw the animals, and that Clarissimns Clusius and Ray, misinformed by them, have affirmed many things of the animal that are inconsistent with truth and autopsy.

1. The animal has no hair at all that can properly be called hair. It has bristles rather, or hollow quills, and these are found only around the mouth and under the feet.

2. The head of this animal is not that of a calf, as Cl. Clusius says; not that of an ox, as Hernandes was pleased to describe it; but in the character of its covering it is like no other animal, but has its own peculiar appearance.

3. The feet are entirely without claws, but skin covers them as it does the bone of an amputated limb, so that the animal moves upon a skin that is rough with bristles.

4. As to the fact that Hernandes attributes to this animal nails like those which men have, in order to make it more like the Platonic man, that is equally false, for the animal has no fingers at all any more than nails, unless perchance the hoof of a horse, to which it bears a certain resemblance, impresses anyone as being like a human nail.

5. And so, by the way, it is evident even from this how much obscurity envelops this subject if we start with false premises and arrive at worse conclusions. For instance, all authors with one consent agree that this animal ascends rivers and feeds upon the grass that it may manage to get along the banks, for they may perhaps have heard from the people that it feeds on herbs; but those are not land herbs, but seaweeds.

Nor does the statement have the appearance of truth, that they are in the habit of lying upon the rocks and of coming up on the land, even if I say nothing of the fact that the structure of the animal is totally unfitted for moving on dry land. Indeed, it happened that as the tide went out the waves receded from under one of the animals sound asleep and left him high and dry upon the shore; but he was helpless and unable to get away, a pitiable object, at the mercy of our cudgels and axes.

That this animal should be tamed seems more likely than do the anecdotes that are given of its remarkable sagacity, since even the untamable can be tamed through its stupidity and greediness. It happened to me on one unlucky occasion that I could watch the habits and ways of these beasts daily for ten months from the door of my hut, and I will briefly note down the observations that I made with great care.

These animals are fond of shallow sandy places along the seashore, but they like especially to live around the mouths of rivers and creeks, for they love fresh running water, and they always live in herds. They keep the young and the half-grown before them while they feed, but they are careful to surround them on the flank and rear and always to keep them in the middle of the herd. When the tide came in they came up so close to the shore that I often hunted them with my stick or lance, and sometimes even stroked their backs with my hand. If they were badly hurt, they did nothing but withdraw to a distance from the shore, and after a short time they would forget their injury and come back. Most commonly whole families live together in one community, the male with one grown female and their tender little offspring. They appear to me to be monogamous. The young are born at any time of year, but most frequently in autumn, as I judged from the new-born little ones that I saw about that time. From this fact, as I noticed that they copulated by preference in the early spring, I concluded that the foetus remained more than a year in the womb. From the shortness of the [uterine] cornua (*ex cornuum brevitate*), and from the fact that there are only two mammae, I infer that they have but one calf, and I have never seen more than one with the mother at a time.

These animals are very voracious and eat incessantly, and because they are so greedy they keep their heads always under water, without regard to life and safety. Hence a man in a boat, or swimming naked, can move among them without danger and select at ease the one of the herd he desires to strike — and accomplish it all while they are feeding. When they raise their noses above the water, as they do every four or five minutes, they blow out the air and a little water with a snort such as a horse makes in blowing his nose. As they feed they move first one foot and then the other, as cattle and sheep do when they graze, and thus with a gentle motion half swim and half walk. Half of the body — the back and sides — projects above the water. While they feed, the gulls are wont to perch upon their backs and to feast upon the vermin that infest their skin, in the same way as crows do upon the lice of hogs and sheep. The manatees do not eat all seaweeds without distinction, but especially (1) *Crispum Brassicae Sabaudicae*, with cancellate leaf [sea-cabbage]; (2) that which has the shape of a club; (3) that which has the shape of an ancient Roman shield; (4) a very long seaweed with a wavy ruffle along the stalk. Where they have stopped, even for a day, great heaps of roots and stems are to be seen cast upon the shore by the waves. When their stomachs are full some of them go to sleep flat on their backs, and go out a distance from the shore that they may not be left on the dry sand when the tide goes out. In winter they are often suffocated by the ice that floats about the shore and are cast upon the beach dead. This also happens when they get caught among the rocks and are dashed by the waves violently upon them. In the winter the animals become so thin that, besides the bones of the spine, all the ribs show. In the spring they come together in the human fashion, and especially about evening in a smooth sea. But before they come together they practice many amorous preludes. The female swims gently to and fro in the water, the male following her. The female eludes him with many twists and turns until she herself, impatient of longer delay, as if tired and under compulsion, throws herself upon her back, when the male, rushing upon her, pays the tribute of his passion, and they rush into each other's embrace.

Their capture used to be effected with a large iron hook whose point resembled an anchor's fluke. The other end was secured by a very long, stout rope to an iron ring. A strong man took this hook and entered the boat with four or five others, and while one held the rudder three or four rowed gently toward the herd. The spearman stood in the prow of the boat holding the hook in his hand, and struck as soon as he was near enough. As soon as this was done, thirty men standing on the shore with the other end of the rope in their hands held the animal, and in spite of its frantic efforts at resistance they dragged him laboriously toward the shore. The boat was held steady by another rope, and the men wore the animal out by constant blows, until, tired and rendered thoroughly passive by the spears, it was finished by their knives and other weapons and drawn to land. Great pieces were cut from the animal while still alive, but all that he did was to work his tail vigorously and to brace himself with his fore feet, so that great pieces of skin were often torn off. Besides, he breathed heavily, as with a groan, and the blood from the wonnded back spurted up like a fountain. As long as he kept his head under water the blood did not flow out, but as soon as he raised his head to breathe the blood leaped forth anew. This happened because the lungs, being situated at the back, were wounded first, and as often as they were filled with air they increased the force of spurting blood. From this I have concluded that the circulation of the blood in this animal, as in the seal, is in a double fashion — in the open air, through the lungs, but under water, through the *foramen ovale* and *ductus arteriosus*, although I did not find both. But I think it happens that they breathe differently from fishes, so that they can better swallow solid food, rather than for the sake of promoting circulation (*propter deglutitionem solidorum potiusquam propter cir culationem promovendam*).

The full-grown, very large animals are more easily taken than the young ones, because the young move about far more vigorously, and even if a whole hook should be fixed in one of them it can get free by tearing the hook out of the skin. We saw this done more than once.

But if one animal is caught with the hook and begins to plunge about rather violently those near him in the herd are thrown into commotion as well and endeavor to assist him. To this end some of them try to upset the boat with their backs, others bear down upon the rope and try to break it, or endeavor to extract the hook from the back of their wounded companion with a blow from their tails, and several times they proved successful. It is a very curious evidence of their nature and of their conjugal affection that when a female was caught the male, after trying with all his strength, but in vain, to free his captured mate, would follow her quite to the shore, even though we struck him many blows, and that when she was dead he would sometimes come up to her as unexpectedly and as swiftly as an arrow. When we came the next day, early in the morning, to cut up the flesh and take it home, we found the male still waiting near his mate; and I saw this again on the third day when I came alone for the purpose of examining the entrails.

As to voice, the animal is dumb and utters no sound, but only breathes heavily and seems to sigh when wounded. I will not venture to assert how much their eyes and ears are worth. Anyway, they see and hear but little, because they keep their heads under water. At all events, the animal himself seems to neglect and despise the use of these organs.

Of all those who have written about the manatee, no one has given a fuller or more careful account than that most curious and painstaking explorer, Captain Dampier, in his travels, published in English in London in 1702. As I read it I could find no fault with it, although a few statements did not correspond with our animal.* For instance, he says that there are two species of manatees, in one of which the eyes are better than the ears, and in the other of which the ears are better than the eyes. What he says about the manner of hunting the animal, namely, that the Americans approach without any noise and without speaking, so as not to frighten the manatee, is no doubt true of places where they are caught in great numbers and have learned by long experience that men are dangerous to them. It was the same way with the otter, seal, and blue fox (*Isatis*), which lived in this desert island and never saw a man before and never were disturbed while lying at their ease. They were slain with no trouble at all when we first came to Bering Island, but now they have become just as wild as those living in Kamchatka, and take flight at once as they discover, not only with their eyes, but even with their sense of smell, the approach of an enemy.

It sometimes occurred that these animals were cast up dead by storms around the cape called Kronotskoi, as well as about Avatcha Bay. Because of the food they eat they are called by the inhabitants, in their language, "*Kapustnik*" (Kraut Esser; weed eaters); this I learned after my return in 1742.

Now, I must tell the uses to which the parts of this animal are put. The skins, which are very thick, firm, and tough, are used by the Americans, according to Hernandes, for the soles of shoes and for belts. I understand that the Tschuktschi use the skins for boats; that they stretch it with sticks and use it in the same way as the Koriaks use the skins of the largest sort of seals, called "*Lachtak.*"

The fat underlies the cuticle and the skin and covers the whole body to the depth of a span, and in some parts is almost 9 inches thick. It is glandulous, stiff, and white, but when exposed to the sun it becomes yellow like May butter (*butyri maialis*). Its odor and flavor are so agreeable that it can not be compared with the fat of any other sea

* It is of course to be remembered that Dampier was speaking of the true manatees *Trichechus inunguis* and *T. latirostris*. [1899 note]

beast. Indeed, it is by far preferable to that of any other quadruped. Moreover, it can be kept a very long time, even in the hottest weather, without becoming rancid or strong. When tried out it is so sweet and fine flavored that we lost all desire for butter. In flavor it approximates nearly the oil of sweet almonds and can be used for the same purposes as butter. In a lamp it burns clear, without smoke or smell. And, indeed, its use in medicine is not to be despised, for it moves the bowels gently, producing no loss of appetite or nausea, even when drunk from a cup; and, in my opinion, it would do calculous persons more good than the masticatory bones or so-called stones (*lapides*) of the manatee. The fat of the tail is harder and stiffer and so more delicate when tried out. The flesh has a grain somewhat tougher and coarser than beef, and is redder than the flesh of land animals; and what is remarkable, even in the hottest days it can be kept in the open air for a very long time without any bad odor, even though all full of worms. I attribute this to the fact that the animal lives entirely upon seaweed and sea plants. These weeds contain a smaller proportion of sulphur and more sea salt and nitre. This salt prevents the loss of sulphur and the softening and decaying of the flesh, preserving it in the same way as salt or brine sprinkled upon meat; but they work even more powerfully, as these salts are more intimately mingled with the substance of the flesh and are combined more permanently with the sulphurous parts (or particles of sulphur?) (*cum sulphureis partibus fortius cohaereant*).

Although the flesh needs to be cooked longer, yet when done it has an excellent taste, not easy to distinguish from that of beef. The fat of the calves resembles fresh lard, so that you can hardly tell the difference; but their flesh is just like veal. When boiled it soon becomes tender, and if the boiling is continued it swells up like young pork so that it takes up twice as much space in the pot as it did before boiling; but the muscles of the abdomen, back, and, sides are far better. The flesh does not really refuse to be salted, as many have thought, but the salt only modifies it, so that it becomes quite like corned beef and very excellent in flavor.

The internal organs—heart, kidneys, and. liver—are very tough, and we did not try to do much with them, because we had a great abundance of meat without.

A full-grown animal weighs about 8,000 pounds, or 80 hundredweight, or 200 Russian "*pud.*" There is so large a number of these ani-

mals about this one island that they would suffice to support all the inhabitants of Kamchatka.

The manatee is infested with a peculiar insect something like a
louse, which is wont to occupy and inhabit in great numbers especially
the wrinkled arms, the udder, the teats, the pudenda, the anus, and the
rough hollows of the skin. When they bore through the cuticle and
the cutis, here and there wart-like prominences are produced by the
lymphatic moisture that exudes. So these insects attract the gulls to
perch upon the backs of the animals and hunt this dainty with their
sharp beaks, thus rendering the animals, which are worried by the vermin, a friendly and welcome service.

These insects are for the most part half an inch long, articulated,
six-footed, translucent, white or yellowish. The head is oblong, sharp,
larger than a millet seed. In front extend two short, jointed little an-
tennae half a line long. In place of a lower mandible it has two slender, two jointed little arms like a shrimp, very sharp and pointed on
the end. Furthermore, in accordance with the number of his feet, he
is composed of six articulations, convex on the back, and one-third of
a line wide. But the ring of the thorax is twice as wide, and they grow
narrower toward the tail. The ring of the thorax resembles the half of
a lentil. On the sides of this a pair of thick claws grows, with two joints
each. Each claw ends in a flexible point, by means of which it holds
fast to the skin of the manatee; the rest of the legs are rather slender, all ending in prickly points, and gradually shorter. The last two
are the shortest, and, growing out from the orbicular ring of the tail,
form the end of the body itself and steer the insect as it moves.

The Sea Bear*

The following is a description of the animal first seen and described by Dampier under the name "sea bear"; called by the Russians "Kot," *gentilibus ad Sinum Penschinicum Tarlatshega*. The description made on the 28th of May, 1742, on Bering Island. The largest weighing about 18-20 Russian "pud" or 800 pounds.[†]

*   *   *   *   *

Habits and Characteristics

Dampier has given us a description of this animal, called *Kot* by the Russians, which is, to be sure, brief and imperfect; but he mentions its characteristics so definitely and plainly and so clearly at first sight that I can not doubt that the animal is his "sea bear."

Report, as I gather from the account of the people, has declared that the sea bear, as it is called by the Rutheni and other people, is different. They say it is an amphibious sea beast very like the bear, but very fierce, both on land and in the water. They told, likewise, that in the year 1736 it had overturned a boat and torn two men to pieces; that they were very much alarmed when they heard the sound of its voice, which was like the growl of a bear, and that they fled from their chase of otter and seals on the sea and hastened back to land. They say that it is covered with white fur; that it lives near the Kuril Islands, and is more numerous toward Japan; that here it is seldom seen. I myself do not know how far to believe this report, for no one has ever seen one, either slain or cast up dead upon the shore.

This is certain, whether we consider the appearance of the body or the habits of the beast, it is more nearly related and more similar to no other land animal than to a bear.

They are never seen in the gulf of the Penshin Sea nor in the land of Kamchatka, nor do they go on shore in the Kuril Islands except very seldom; they are not taken except on three Kuril Islands, and

---

* or fur seal.

† The Miller translation omits 15 pages of measurements and descriptions of the external and internal parts.

from there to the mouth of the river of Kamchatka, in the so-called Bobrovi [sea otter] Sea, from latitude 50° to 56° N. These bears pass by the Kuril Islands in the early spring, and in September they are taken in small numbers about the mouth of the river called Shupanova and from there to Cape Kronotski in greater numbers. Here, to be sure, between the two capes, Kronotski and Shipunski, the sea is quieter and there are more inlets and recesses; hence the animals delay here longer as they pass by and more of them are caught. Almost all that are caught in the spring are females, and have the young almost ready for birth within them. The foetuses, when removed, are called "*Vipo-rotki.*" All that are found are put on the market. They are no longer to be seen anywhere from the first of June to the end of August, when, with their young, they return to the south. For many years these migratory animals have been a source of wonder and speculalation to the people who have been interested in hunting them. For, whence did these animals come in early spring? Whither were these very fat, these pregnant beasts, going in countless droves? What are the reasons for this migration? Why do they return with their offspring in the fall so thin, dry, and weak? And whither are they going?

From the fact that the animals come very fat from the south in early spring and return thither in the fall, it was naturally inferred that they had taken no long jonrney, and that their winter quarters could not be very far distant, else they would become too thin upon the way. And from the fact that they were all going toward the east and were never seen beyond Cape Kronotski or the mouth of the Kamchatka Kiver, either going east or returning home, they concluded that there must necessarily be some land, either island or mainland, near the land of Kamchatka and in a line with Cape Kronotski.

Among amphibious sea beasts these are the migratory animals, like geese, swans, and other sea birds, or like catanadromous trout among fishes; the blue foxes, hares, and mice occupy this place among quadrupeds. Now the migration of the blue fox is undertaken because food becomes scarce. Birds and fishes migrate to lay their eggs or to indulge undisturbed their sexual instincts, and, because their strength is reduced or their feathers shed, and hence they are unable to flee from their foes until these can grow once more, solitary places are chosen by birds and quiet lakes by fishes. Accordingly, for a similar reason, these northern places are chosen by the sea bears; and these desert islands, lying in great numbers between America and Asia from 50° to 56° north latitude, are chosen for the following reasons.

That the mothers may bear their young there upon the land and after parturition recruit their strength; further, that the young may there be brought up and nourished and may grow strong enough in three months to follow their parents home in the autumn. The pups are fed with their mother's milk for two months. The mothers have nipples corresponding in form, size, and position with those of the sea otter, and they are situated near the pudenda. They bear one pup at a birth, very seldom two. After parturition they gnaw the umbilical cord off from the pups with their teeth, as dogs do, and lick it till it is dry, so as to keep the blood soft until it heals; and they devour the afterbirth greedily. The pups are born with their eyes open, and their eyes are as large as those of a calf. When they are born they have thirty-two teeth started out on a level with the gums; but there are four larger canine teeth, ferocious and suitable for battle, still hidden in the gums. These come out after the fourth day. When the pups are born they are covered with shining black fur all over. But the fourth or fifth day after birth the fur under the front legs changes color perceptibly and takes on the color of the hair of Pliny's goat; and after a month the belly and sides become speckled with an intermixture of hairs of the same color. At birth the males are much larger and darker, and in the years that follow they get a blacker coat than the females. These latter become almost wholly ashy gray, but have rusty spots under the forelegs. The females differ so much from the males in size, weight, and strength, that a careless observer might almost take them for a different species, so timid and so little ferocious are they.

The parents love their young exceedingly. The females, after parturition, lie in crowds upon the shore with their pups and spend much time in sleeping. The pups, however, directly in the first days play together like children, and imitate their parents in playing at copulation, and practice fighting until one throws the other to the ground. When the father sees this he rises up with a growl and hastens to separate the combatants, kisses the victor, licks him with his tongue, tries with his mouth to throw him upon the ground, and makes vigorous demonstrations of his love for the youngster, who struggles bravely against it. In short, he rejoices that he has a son worthy of himself. But they are less fond of the lazy and ease-loving pups. Hence some of the young are always near the father, others near the mother. The males are polygamous; one often has eight, fifteen, or even fifty wives. He guards them with anxious jealousy, and goes into a rage if another male comes ever so little too near.

Although many thousands of them lie upon the shore together, yet it may always be observed that they are separated into families — the one male lies with his wives, his sons, and daughters, as also his yearling sons who are not yet old enough to have a harem. One family often numbers as many as 120. For this reason also they swim in the sea in shoals.

All the married ones are vigorous, but the aged and those that are too old for the warfare incident to keeping up a harem, or that are driven to it by impotence or the voluntary desertion of their wives, lead a monastic life, and pass it constantly in fasting and sleep. These married ones are the fattest of all, and without the females they come first to the island, like scouts. All the males have a strong odor, but theirs is the worst. These old animals are very cross and very savage. They live a whole month in one place without food or drink; they sleep all the time, but rage with exceeding fierceness at all who pass by. Indeed, they are so very fierce and jealous that they would a hundred times rather die than give up their place. And so if they see a man they go out to get in his way and prevent his passing; one of the others meanwhile gets his place and is ready to fight with him. When we were obliged to come into conflict with them because of the necessity of continuing our journey, we threw great stones at them. They in turn would rage at the stone thrown at them just as a dog would, and start up in defiance and fill the air with their terrible roaring. What we first attempted was to knock out their eyes and break their teeth with stones; even though wounded and blind they would not give up their place or dare to leave it; for if one of them went even a pace away, so many enemies would rise up and attack him with their teeth as he fled that he should not leave his place, that even if he escaped our hands he would be torn to pieces by his fellows. Indeed, if one leaves his place, the rest run up to prevent his flight; one attacks the other on suspicion of wishing to flee, and from a single attack so many duels originate that oftentimes for 2 or 3 furlongs by the seashore you can see nothing but duels, battles, and a thousand sights absurd but bloody, accompanied by a terrific roaring and growling. While they fight with one another they let us alone, and we are able to pass by unmolested. If two fight against one, another comes to his aid, for they can not bear to see an unequal combat. When there is fighting going on, others who are swimming in the sea lift up their heads to see the outcome of the contest, and finally they are worked into such a rage themselves that they come on shore and mix in crowds with the combatants and make the sight more awful. I often went with my Cossack and attacked one on purpose and knocked out his eyes; and when I had done that I pelted four or five others with stones. When these pursued me I took refuge near the one I had blinded. As he could not see but heard his brothers in pursuit and did not know whether they were fleeing before us or pursuing us, he would attack his fellows. Meanwhile, quite at my ease, I would sit down in some high place and watch them fighting together for some hours. The blind one would attack all that came near, whether enemies or friends, and was pursued by all as a common foe. If he fled to the sea he was pulled out again, and on land was torn by their constant blows until he lost all his strength, and falling down breathed out his angry soul amid constant groans, and became a prey to the hungry droves of blue foxes which attacked him with their teeth as he lay there still breathing.

While two often fight for an hour, they make a truce, and both lie down near one another, panting to get their breath. When they are recovered they both get up and in gladiatorial fashion take a certain place and refuse to leave it as long as the fighting. continues. They duck their heads and strike back, and one tries to ward off the blows of the other. As long as they are evenly matched they strike only with their front flippers, but as soon as one gets the advantage of his adversary he tears him with his teeth and jaws, shakes him, and throws him down. Then the others, who have meantime been mere spectators, seeing this, hurry up to assist the weaker one, as if they were umpires in the fight. With their teeth they inflict wounds as large and cruel as if they were made with a saber. At the end of July a sea bear is seldom seen that is not marked with a wound. After a battle the first thing they do is to go into the water and bathe their bodies.

They fight mostly for one of three reasons: (1) The most bitter warfare is about their wives; trouble begins when one steals those of another, or even tries to take the grown daughters from the father's family. But the females get up at once and follow the one that comes out ahead. (2) They fight for their place if one takes the place of another, or if the space is too small and another, out of lust, gets too near and excites his suspicion. (3) They fight for right and justice, to settle disputes.

They are very fond of their wives and their young, and are much feared by both. They get in a towering rage with their young for the most trivial causes and practice a tyrants right.

Often we entered the harem and stole the pups. In these cases, when flight was possible, if the mother through fear left her pups and did not snatch them up in her mouth and take them with her, but left them where we could get them, the male without entering into any quarrel with us snatched the female up in his teeth, lifted her up high, and threw her in a rage two or three times against the rocks with such violence that she lay still as if dead. But when her strength returned she would crawl like a worm as a suppliant to his feet, and kiss him, and shed tears in such quantities that they ran down on her breast as from an alembic and made it all wet. For a time he would walk back and forth roaring and rolling his eyes terribly, and would shake his head from side to side like a bear; but at length when he saw that we were going to go away with the pups, he would weep in the same way as the female, and just as copiously, so as to flood his whole breast, even to his feet, with tears. The same thing occurs when he suffers grievous wounds or some severe injury which he can not avenge. I have seen captive seals weep in a similar way.

A second reason why the sea bears in early spring go east to these desert islands is doubtless this. By rest, sleep, and a three months' fast, they must rid themselves of their burdensome fat, in the same way as land bears do in winter. For during the months of June, July, and August, they do nothing except sleep upon land, or lie at ease in one spot like a rock, and look at each other, roar, kiss, and stretch, taking neither food nor drink. One in particular I noticed lying in the same spot for a whole month. Although at different times I dissected the old males, yet I found nothing at all in their stomachs except froth and gastric juice, and no faeces in the bowels. Furthermore, I noted that meanwhile the layers of fat wasted away more and more, the size of the body becoming diminished and the skin becoming so loose that it hung like a sack and swayed with each motion of the body. The younger ones that are not so fat begin to cohabit about the first of

THE BEASTS OF THE SEA

July; they are active and run here and there, living on land and in the sea by turns. This fact convinced me still further that in accordance with his nature I should call this animal a bear.

They cohabit after the manner of the human kind, the female below and the male above, and especially near evening time do they desire to indulge their passion. An hour before, male and female cast themselves into the sea and swim around quietly together. Then they come back together, and the female lies flat on her back while the male comes up out of the sea upon her. He seizes her in his arms and indulges his passion with the greatest heat. During the coition he presses the female down and buries her in the sand by his weight so that only her head sticks out, and he himself digs into the sand with his front feet, so that he presses down and touches the female with his whole belly. For this they choose a sandy spot upon the very shore, where the waves come even to the place. So absorbed are they and so forgetful of themselves that I could stand near them for more than a quarter of an hour without being observed. And I should not have been seen even then had I not struck the male a blow, whereupon with a great uproar he attacked me so wrathfully that I got away with difficulty. But nevertheless when I gained an eminence from which I could look down he went on for another quarter of an hour with what he had begun.

These animals have three different kinds of speech. To pass away the time while they lie upon the land they cry out, and their voice is not at all different from the lowing of cows when deprived of their calves. In battle they roar and growl like a bear, and if they get the victory they utter a very sharp and often repeated note like our common crickets. But when wounded and overcome by their enemies they groan terribly or hiss like a cat or sea otter.

When they come out of the sea they shake their bodies and wipe off their breasts with their back flippers, and smooth their fur. The male places the tip of his lips to those of the female as if to kiss her. When the sun shines clear in the sky they lie down and raise their back flippers in the air and move them in the same way as a dog wags his tail. They lie sometimes on their back and sometimes on their belly like a dog, sometimes curled up in a ball, sometimes stretched out on one side with their front flippers resting on the side. But although they sleep soundly, and though a man may approach softly, nevertheless they are speedily aware of his presence and get up, whether informed by hearing or the sense of smell I know not.

The very large old ones never run away from a man or a crowd of men, but prepare at once for battle. Nevertheless, I have seen whole herds put to flight if a man whistle. The females flee in haste, and likewise whole droves of adult males, even many thousands, are driven in headlong flight to the sea, if suddenly, when they feel secure, they are attacked with a great noise. But when, as often, we drove many thousands of them before us into the ocean, those that were swimming accompanied us constantly as we walked along the shore, gazing in wonder upon their unusual guests.

They swim so rapidly that in an hour they can easily swim two German miles. If they are wounded at sea with a harpoon they draw the boat with the hunter after them so swiftly that the boat seems to fly, and they often overturn the boat and drown the hunter unless the steersman prevents it by watching and skillfully directing his course; they swim with the back sloping, and the front flippers are never seen, but the back ones sometimes project up from the water. On account of the open *foramen* they stay a long time under water. But they afterwards come up to breathe, with their strength much exhausted; they delight to swim around near the shore and swim now prone and now on their backs, but not far under water, so that I was always able to make out their course. They often raise their hind flippers out of the water. When they have breathed enough, or when they first start into the water from the land, they plunge into the water head first like a wheel, as do almost all the larger sea beasts – the otter, the lion, the balaena orca, and the porpoise.

When they climb a rock, they take hold of it with their front flippers as seals do, and drag the rest of their body behind them, bending the back like a bow and holding the head low, to give elasticity to the body. In swiftness they almost if not quite excel the swiftest runner, and the females are especially fast. There is no doubt that many of us would have been killed by them if their legs were worth as much on land as they are in water. And, indeed, it is not wise to fight with them even in a large level place, for there one can get away with difficulty. Steep places were always our refuge of safety, because they can not climb up them. They sometimes laid siege to me for more than six hours, and at length compelled me, at very great peril of my life, to ascend a precipice, and in that way to escape from the infuriated beasts.

If I were required to state how many I saw on Bering Island I should truthfully say that I could not guess — they were countless, they covered the whole shore. Not infrequently they obliged me and my Cossack, in our rambles this way and that through the entire island, to leave the shore and prosecute our journey with difficulty over the tops of the hills.

The sea otters are very much in fear of the sea bears, and very seldom come in among them, and it is the same with the seals. But the sea lions live among them in great herds and are much feared by them. They always have the best places. The sea bears do not like to stir up quarrels when the sea lions are present for fear they have these savage beasts as umpires; for they run up immediately, as I have sometimes seen. So also they dare not try to prevent their females from playing with the sea lions.

And, by the way, this is a curious fact, that the sea bears are not found everywhere on the shores of their islands, as are the sea cows, the seals, the otter, and the sea lions, but only on the southern shore, which faces Kamchatka. The reason of this is obvious — for they see this part of the island first when they come on their journey eastward from Cape Kronotski. They are not found in the northern part unless they have strayed there by mistake.

Now about the hunting of these animals. Those that we first blinded on land with stones were afterward dispatched with clubs without any artifice. But the beasts are so tenacious of life that two or three men beating only their heads with clubs could scarcely kill them with 200 blows, and frequently would have to rest and refresh themselves two or three times. When the cranium is broken into little bits and almost all the brains have gushed out, and all the teeth have been broken, he still attacks them with his flippers and keeps on fighting. I have purposely broken the skull and put out the eyes of one and then left him, and afterwards for more than two weeks he still stood alive and unmoved, like a statue, in the same place.

In the sea around Kamchatka they very seldom come ashore on the mainland, but they are wounded at sea by the natives with an iron spear called "*nosok*" which detaches from the handle and remains in the body, and this iron part of the spear, because inside it is oblique to the wound, sticks fast. It is bound to a stout thong, the other end of which is held by those sitting in the boat. But the wounded animal flees very swiftly like an arrow, and takes the boat and men along with him, until he pauses, worn out and exhausted with loss of blood. As soon as he pauses they draw him up to them by the thong and pierce him with spears, and if he attempts to upset the boat they crush his front flippers and his head with axes and clubs, lift him dead into the boat, and hasten home. By preference in spring they kill the pregnant females and the young males. But they dare not attack the large, old males, but when they see one they say *"Sipang"* (the devil), for they mean by that to call the big fellow evil and destructive. So likewise they say if they see a sea lion or a very large sea bear on land when they have no companion or weapons.

Very many sea bears die a natural death from old age on this island every year, and as many more fall in battle and die from the wounds that they have received; so that in some parts the whole shore is covered with bones and skulls, as if great battles had been fought there.

I can not omit to mention that these animals have a very large thymus gland, composed of many little glands, and rolled up in a membranous sac. I have made an incision into a branch of the main artery of the lungs, and when I inserted a little tube and blew in with my mouth I discovered that not only the ventricles of the heart but also the thymus gland swelled up. I would rather not suggest what others may conclude in regard to this, unless I could make many more experiments on other sea beasts.

Here, at the end, I will mention that it is a very curious thing what the explorer, Dampier, says of the Island Ferdinand (Juan Fernandez), below 36° south latitude, he asserts that there upon the land he found the whole shore covered with countless herds of seals, sea lions, and sea bears, in the same way as we found it in Bering Island. This does not lead me to believe that these animals come hither from those Southern latitudes, for this distance would be far too great, but I gather from it two facts: first, that the sea beasts of the southern hemisphere are the same, or not very different, from those of the northern in about the same longitude; and, second, it is credible that our sea bears spend the winter at about the same degree of north latitude. Perchance some time fate will grant that since we have found their summer camping ground others may somewhere discover their winter home; if this be not the land called "*Compagnie land*" perchance it may be a land lying not far away and some time to be discovered.

I have had two pictures made, of which the former represents a male resting on a rock, as they are generally seen; and the second, a smaller female lying upon her back. I have her represented in this position chiefly for the reason that the shape of the hind leg may appear, and this could not be brought out true to nature if she were in sitting position.

Comm. Nov. Ac. Sc. Petr. Tom. II. Tab. XV.

Fig. 2.

Fig. 1.

As to style and arrangement of matter, pressure of duties does not permit me to spend too much time in perfecting any one thing, unless I am to allow many things to go to waste upon my hands. I therefore set out my porridge in carefully made earthen vessels. If the vessel is an offense to any one, he will perform for me and others a most friendly service if he will pour it all into a gold or silver urn. As to the fact that I have noted the minutest circumstances, I did it for this reason: that I might omit nothing that I learned from careful watching. For the rest, I guarantee that I say nothing that is not most true; an account can always be made shorter, but not longer or fuller, if it has been from the outset restricted within rather narrow limits.

The Sea Lion

Description of the beast of the sea named by Dampier the sea lion, by the Kurils, Kamchatkans, and Russians "Siwutscha." Described on Bering Island the 20th of June 1742.*

*   *   *   *   *

Habits and characteristics

These beasts are indeed terrible to look upon when alive; and they far surpass the sea bear in strength and size as well as in endurance of the different parts. They are hard to overcome and fight most viciously when cornered. They also give to the eyes and mind the impression of a lion. Nevertheless, they fear so much the very sight of man that if they see one even at a distance they rush in headlong flight from the land into the sea. But if, when they are sound asleep, a man comes up near and wakes them by a blow from his stick or by a loud noise) they take to flight at once, panting like a furnace, and with their limbs shaking so with fear that they can not control them. But if one of them is cornered and all chance for flight is shut off he turns against his enemy with a great roar, shakes his head in wrath, rages, cries out, and puts even the bravest man to flight. The first time that I tried this experiment was almost the last of me. On this account this animal is never hunted at sea by the Kamchatkan tribes, because he overturns the boat of the hunters and slays them most savagely. Nor does anyone dare engage him even on land in open battle, but he is caught by guile when off his guard and quite at ease, or even sound asleep. When the beast is asleep on land, the hunter who has most confidence in his strength and swiftness, creeps silently up to it with the wind in his face and plunges into it under its fore flippers an iron or bone spear called a "*nosok*." It is made to fly out of its socket and is fastened to a thong made from the skin of this very animal. The other hunters keep the thong, which is wound several times around a rock or a stake driven deep into the ground. While the beast that has been wounded and

---

* The Miller translation here omits 2 pages of introductory description.

aroused attempts to get away, the other men shoot arrows at it from a distance, or transfix it with a second spear fastened to a thong. At length when its strength is gone they pierce it with spears and kill it with clubs. But when they attack it they attack it asleep on the shore where there are few rocks; they shoot poisoned arrows, and then run away. The animal is compelled by the poison to come on shore, as the salt sea water increases the pain of the wounds; and then, if the place is a convenient one, he is stabbed, or otherwise, if left to himself, he will die of the poison in twenty-four hours. All who have the skill and daring to hunt this beast, and who have killed many, are held in great honor by their fellows, and are regarded as heroes and braves. Accordingly the love of glory, as well as the excellence of the flesh, turns many to the hunt and makes them ready for hazardous enterprises. They often load their boats with two or even three of these animals, till they threaten to sink in the water. But they are so skillful that this seldom happens in the smooth sea, even though the rim of the boat may be even with the surface of the water. They consider it a great disgrace if, through fear of death, they abandon the quarry that they have once secured, so that if their hands should not avail to bail out the water they would sink. To hunt this beast the bravest men go out to sea in their light canoes four or five German miles to the uninhabited island called Alait. And it not infrequently happens that the sailors without a compass are taken by a contrary wind four, five, or even eight days out to sea without anything to eat, and see neither island nor mainland, and have only the rising and setting of the sun and moon to direct them.

The blubber, as well as the sweet flesh, is well flavored and highly prized, and the gelatinous flippers are considered a prime delicacy. The fat is not greasy, like that of seals and whales, but is stiff, and resembles that of sea bears in color, but not in flavor and smell. The fat of the young is sweeter than mutton tallow and resembles the marrow of leg bones. From the skin they make thongs, the soles of shoes, and even shoes themselves and leggins.

They are polygamous. One male has two, three, or four females. The pups are born on land about the beginning of June — one only at a birth, and are suckled by their mothers. They come together in August and September, hence the young remains in the womb nine months, as indeed seems reasonable. They copulate like the sea bears.

The males hold the females in great respect and do not treat them so harshly as the sea bears do their wives. They delight exceedingly in the caresses of the females and count their affection worthy of much more demonstrative return. The males, like the females, have a very indifferent love for the pups. The mothers when asleep sometimes crush the young at their udders by their weight and kill them, as I have often seen, and they were not the least bit disturbed when, as often, I cut the throats of the young, even before the eyes of their parents and threw the entrails to them. The pups are not so lively and active as those of the sea bears, but sleep all the time or play a little in a lazy way, and indulge in amatory sports. At eventide the mothers with the young go out into the sea and swim quietly near the shore. When the pups get tired of swimming they are wont to perch upon the backs of their mothers and rest. But the mother rolls over like a wheel and shakes the lazy pups off, and accustoms them to swimming. As an experiment I have thrown young sea bears and equally young sea lions into the water; but they were so far from being able to swim or to use their flippers well that they beat the waves irregularly with their flippers and hurried to the shore. The pups are twice as large as those of sea bears.

Although these animals are exceedingly afraid of man, yet I have seen them grow used to him and become tame by meeting him frequently without injury, and especially at that time when the pups had not yet learned to swim easily. I lived a season in the midst of a herd of them, and for six whole days on a spot above them, where from my hut I watched their habits carefully. They lay around me in every direction; they watched my fire and what I did, and did not run away any longer even when I walked around among them and took their pups and killed them and examined them. They practiced coition, fought jealously for their wives and for the best places, and fought most bitterly in just the same way and with the same motions and the same heat as the sea bears do. One from whom a female had been taken fought with all the rest for three whole days, and was wounded all over in more than a hundred places. The sea bears never mingle in their fights, but if a quarrel arises they run away, looking all around them. They yield them the choice of places and allow their females and pups to indulge in various sports, and dare not object. As far as possible they avoid all dealings with the sea lions, but these, uninvited and unwelcome, often mix in their quarrels. The old and decrepit among them grow white around the head, and beyond all doubt these beasts are very long-lived. They scratch their ears and head with their hind flippers, as the bears do, and stand, swim, lie down, and walk in the same way. They low like cows and the young bleat like sheep, and while I was among them it seemed to me as if I were playing shepherd and were mingling with herds of cattle. The old and worn-out emit an odor, but far milder and less offensive than that of the sea bears. They are found in this island in spring, as well as in winter and summer, but only in certain parts — those that are rocky and near precipices. Nevertheless, others come here every year along with the sea bears. I have seen them in great numbers along the American shores. They are found in Kamchatka almost all the time. They do not go above 56° north latitude. They are hunted a great deal near Cape Kronotski and around the island Ostrovnaia, around Avatcha Gulf, and from here as far as Cape Lopatka. They are found in the Kuril Islands and almost as far as Matmej Island. Captain Spangberg on his chart has named a certain island from the number of these animals that he found upon it, and from a cliff overhanging their city, the "Palace of Sivutch." The sea lion is never seen in the Penshin Sea. The reasons why these beasts come hither in June, July, and August, are for quiet, for parturition, for rearing and teaching the pups, and for copulation. Before and after this period they are found in greater numbers on the shores of Kamchatka.

As to the food of these beasts, they prey upon fish and seal especially, and also upon otter and other sea animals. The old ones eat little or nothing at all in June and July, but take their ease and sleep, and at the same time become very thin.

The Sea Otter*

* * * * *

Habits and Characteristics

These animals are very beautiful, and because of their beauty they are very valuable, as one may well believe of a skin the hairs of which, an inch or an inch and a half in length, are very soft, very thickly set, jet black and glossy. The soft uuderfur also among the longer hairs is black; but the tips, or the hairs from the middle on, are black, while the bases or roots are whitish, lustrous like silk, and silvery. The most valuable skins are almost perfectly black; others are found with silvery fur shining quite white all over, but they occur very rarely. Although as time goes on they change the color of their hair, they are still much more constant than the sables, and sable skins never shine with so deep a natural blackness as the otters. The one thing to be deplored is that the skin is too thick and heavy, and for that reason is less pleasing to the eyes of the gentler sex; for the skin of an adult otter weighs, on an average, 3½ pounds.

Rarely is an otter caught that is black all over; the head of the best grade of otters is silvery gray; the cheaper grade of otter has a head of a tawny color and yellowish fur; and the lowest grade of otter is that which has no long hair, and is clad only in short, dirty-gray fur. With these animals matters stand like this: the skins of certain animals always grow red hairs, rarely very long, while the animals themselves are stupid, sluggish, surly, sleepy; they lie forever asleep upon the icy rocks; they move slowly, and can be captured without any painstaking or ingenuity, as if they knew that because of the inferiority of their hides they were not very seriously exposed to death. Many of them, however, have most beautiful tails, covered with long, black fur. From these considerations I have come to two conclusions. (1) That the skins of sluggish animals are overgrown with only short hair, for the simple reason that in summer time, while they roll about in the sand, the

---

* The Miller translation omits 15 pages of measurements and descriptions of the external and internal parts.

longer hairs are worn off by the constant friction, and in the winter, while they lie upon the damp ice, the longer hairs stick fast to the ice, and are pulled off when the animal moves. This I have seen with my own eyes. (2) That black hair, through the influence of air and sunlight, grows lighter and feebler, and so the tail, as it is curled under the lying animal, is less exposed to friction and to the rays of the sun, and so preserves the original blackness and length of hair. The more active and cunning and fleet the animals are, the more beautiful is the fur with which they are covered, and again, unlike the others, they are captured but rarely, and that only by well-laid snares. Such animals are so careful about their own safety that if they come out on dry land alone to sleep, they look around very carefully, and, inasmuch as their eyes are not very strong when on land, they turn their noses in every direction before they go to. sleep, to make sure that no man is in the neighborhood — and then, even though they perceive no sign whatever of danger, they do not get far away from the sea. They often wake up with a start, look around, and never sleep very soundly. But if whole herds sleep together on the land, the finest looking leaders [of the herd] stand on sentinel duty, and arouse the rest if any danger threatens.

The skins of females can be distinguished from those of males at the very first sight, because they have shorter, finer, more beautiful hairs on their backs and longer ones on the belly; the flesh of the females is more tender, more savory, and more delicious because of the distribution of the fat. In the former respect they are different from quadrupeds and birds, for in these classes it is the males that are covered with the more beautiful hair and feathers and the brighter colors.

They do change their hair, however, like land animals and birds, but with this two-fold difference: some lose their hair in the months of July and August, but they lose very little of it; the others change their color somewhat and come out a darker gray, and are for that reason called by the Russians and merchants "Letnie Bobry," and are sold at a smaller price. The most prized skins are those which are taken from animals in March, April, and May.

The adult males are called "*Bobry*," the females, "*Matka*," and the one-year-olds, which have taken on the soft, short fur, "*Koschloki*"; the cubs are called "*Medviedki*," or "little bears," because they have very long, thin, tawny hair like bears; their skins can scarcely be distinguished from the skins of the young bear, but after five months they lose their hair, and then they are called *"Koschloki,"* as intermediating between the cubs and the one-year-olds, and are then covered only with soft, downy fur.

Upward of fifteen years ago, the finest skins were exchanged by the natives in the land of Kamchatka for knives and firearms, and were sold by Russian merchants for 5 or 6 rubles; those of medium quality sold for 4 rubles; those from the Yakut sold for 8 or 10 rubles. But ever since the Chinese began to appreciate and earnestly to covet these wares the finest skins of the adult animal were sold even in the land of Kamchatka for 25 and 30 rubles; those of medium quality for 17, while 1-year-olds (those called *"Koschloki"*) brought 8 rubles, and cubs 1 ruble. Tails were held at a particularly high price, and were purchased for 1½ or even 2 rubles, and were much sought after for caps and mittens.

Very few are brought to Russia; almost all are taken to China, where the best ones command a price of 70 and 80 rubles. In 1735 and 1736 they were quite ready to offer 20 rolls of *"Kitaika"* for one skin, while the Russians on their return to Irkutsk obtained for it 100 rubles.

These skins, moreover, being rather heavy, are for that reason dearer to the Chinese than the skins of sables and foxes, and they are better suited to increase the weight of the too light silk gowns. In addition to their beauty they make the silk fit more closely to the body and resist the wind better; and for those reasons the Chinese make of this fur borders of a hand's breadth and put them around their robes on every side; and this has become the fashion also with both sexes, not among the tribes of Kalmuc and Siberia only, but also in Russia. In the land of Kamchatka nothing is considered a finer adornment than a dress sewed up like a sack (a *"Parka"* they call it), made out of the white skins of reindeer fawns (called *"Püschiki"*) and having a border of sea otter fur around it. Mittens and caps are also made of sea otter fur.

In addition to their weight, these skins have also this disadvantage, that they retain too little heat about the body and become moist, although, because of their thickness, they do afford excellent protection against the violence of the wind.

Up to a few years ago the people there also used to make their clothes out of those skins, as they did long ago out of the skins of foxes and sables (*Zobelae*), but that custom has gone out of date now that their value has increased so much, and they are not very much aggrieved at that change of fashion, for the people there have always looked on dog skins as warmer, more beautiful, and more lasting.

The hides of the cubs have this advantage, that they heat the body less than fox skins do.

These animals are captured only on the shore of Kamchatka, from 50° to 56° north latitude. They are never seen in the Penshin Sea, nor are they observed to go beyond the third Kuril Island. From this fact, and from the hunting of the animal, the ocean from the neighborhood of Lopatka to the Promontory of Kronotski has received the name of "Bobrovi Sea." For a long time back it has been believed by the people, as well as by Russians, and asserted that this animal is not an Asiatic, but a stranger in that region and a foreigner from other lands that lie quite near Kamchatka, where they are taken every year. When the east wind blows for two days together in the winter time, they are floated over with the ice on which they have been lying, and so are caught. Those which escape death in the winter stay in the summer about the rugged and rocky shores of Kamchatka and the Kuril Islands, give birth to their young, and remain there; for they have not the strength to swim away, and, on account of the *foramen ovale* of the heart, they can not while swimming over the sea seek their food in its depths; neither can they hold out against hunger for three or four days.

The hunting of the otter is on this wise: if the winter has been cold and great quantities of ice are repeatedly blown over, there will be an abundance of sea otter not only in winter, but also, from those that survive, in the summer; and, on the other hand, from the year 1740 to 1743 there was no cold weather in this locality, no ice could be frozen about the shores and brought over there, and so the otter were few and the hunting exceedingly limited.

The region famous for the hunting of the otter twenty years ago extended from the mouth of the Kamchatka to the Tchaschma, and was more renowned for that than any other place; now, however, it is but little and rarely used. Hunters came in greater numbers about the Promontory of Kronotski, which has come to be most frequented next after the mouth of the river Kamchatka; but there also the catch has grown smaller. About Ostrovnaia, the Gulf of Avatcha, the Promontory of Lopatka, and the first three Kuril Islands they are now caught

in much greater numbers than before. The Penschin Sea they do not
enter, although crabs and other shellfish are to be found there in at
least as great if not greater numbers than on the Kamchatkan shore.
But why they do not go beyond the first three Kuril Islands, although
they might easily pass from one to the other and so on clear to Japan,
admits of a three-fold explanation. (1) Because the sea lions and sea
bears, inhabiting the desert islands in very great numbers, devour the
sea otter and injure them in every possible manner, the latter are very
much afraid of them and are driven away. (2) There is never any ice in
those regions, and so no sea otter are ever brought. (3) The distance
between America and the farther Kuril Islands is very great, and there
are no islands in between, and so these animals cannot reach them by
swimming. Besides, these creatures are not naturally of a roving dis-
position but if they might find a suitable place designed, as it were, for
them, even so the inhabitants of the first islands are so bent on hunting them that those which have managed to escape in winter rarely escape in summer. They hunt the otter in all seasons, but in most diverse
manner according to the demands of the season. They are captured
in greatest numbers in winter, particularly in the months of February,
March, and April, but their capture is made at the expense of tremen-
dous exertion, great daring, and not infrequently loss of human life.
When in the months before mentioned the east wind blows for two or
three days in succession, a vast quantity of ice is carried over from the
American shore; the ice comes over even more quickly if it has been
carried away in the autumn and held in the channel between the islands. While the wind blows, the hunters lie in wait in their straw-cov-
ered huts; the ice drifts in in so great quantities that it fills the surface
of the sea for several miles out from land in the region of the Kuril
Islands, and oftentimes connects the Promontory of Lapatka with
the first island. Then the hunters, arming themselves with clubs and
knives, put on their snowshoes (called *"lapki"*), and either alone or at-
tended by dogs go out upon the ice. With their clubs they kill the otter they find in a few moments, moving continually the while that they
may not break the ice. They have the skins carefully pulled off, and
leave the carcasses, if they be too far from the shore. Meanwhile the
dogs hunt out others. When the otter catches sight of the dog and the
dog stops, the otter is brought terrified to bay, and attempts to hide,
until the hunter, following the footprints of the dog, comes upon his

quarry and dispatches it. So eagerly do they pursue the hunt that they often go out so far upon the ice that they get out of sight of land.

If, as often happens, the ice is brought in with a gale or tempest and a heavy fall of snow, the catch, is even larger, but fraught with greater danger; for when the hunters can not look ahead nor see the holes in the ice at their feet, they must follow their dog or mere blind chance. This most venturesome chase can not be witnessed from the land without terror. The ice rises and falls with the waves; the hunters walk now upon a mountain which was but a moment before a valley or a deep pit; again they are lifted up on high, and again they sink and disappear from sight. But the best and easiest hunting takes place when the ice remains on the shore for a long time; for while the tempest lasts, the otter, not knowing whether they are on the floating ice or on the land, go inland 5, 10, and even 15 furlongs. For they are misled by the roaring of the wind in the trees and bushes and think they are going toward the sea, and that what they hear is the roar of the waves. In this way a single huntsman often kills as many as thirty or forty or more, and saves the meat as well as the skin.

While the people hunt upon the ice, they are generally very careful to observe the winds, for fear that by adverse winds they be carried, as not infrequently happens, out into the open sea. It is not a rare thing for them to float up and down with the ice upon the waves for three, four, five, and even six days, and then, with favoring fortune and favoring winds, to be brought in again and come safely to shore. When the wind blows from the other quarter the ice is drifted away. If it drifts along the shore, the hunters follow the ice continually, for while the ice is drifting away, whether by day or by night, the otter try to get back upon it again, and so the latter part of the hunt is often richer than the beginning. The hunters wear snowshoes, in order that the ice, which is often very thin, may bear their weight, and keep them from breaking through. Each shoe is from 5 to 6 feet long, 8 inches wide, and is fastened to the foot with straps.

As this hunt takes place upon the ice, it is considered good news all through the Kuril Islands, Lopatka, Kronotski, and Avatcha that the ice has come. Moreover, besides the otter, seals also and sea lions are brought in upon the ice.

The hunting of the otter is planned for in the winter time, because the colder, windier, and stormier the winter the greater the catch, and the milder the winter the poorer the catch. Although in the years 1740, 1741, and 1742 great quantities of ice with great numbers of otter drifted in, still the catch was very insignificant; but the reason was that the ice was very thin and would not hold the hunters.

In summer the otter are caught in four ways. (1) While lying upon their backs asleep at sea they are speared from boats with harpoons. (2) Even when awake they may be driven about in the sea by two boats until they are tired out and then speared, for they can not live under-water for more than two minutes without breathing. If pursued mod-erately, therefore, they swim along and soon get so out of breath that they can flee no farther and are forced to stop. (3) When the tide is out they take refuge on the rocks that rise up above the surface of the sea. There they sleep and are killed by the hunters with clubs. Before the advent of the Russians they used in the same way to come out on land to sleep on the shores of Kamchatka and the Kuril Islands; but ever since they began to be hunted for their skins to satisfy the ava-rice of man they are never caught upon the mainland, or very rarely, when they have come there unaware. (4) They are caught in nets. The nets are spread above the water and tied with stones to hold them firmly in position in not very deep places, where sea weed grows in great quantities, for the otter feed upon shellfish and crustaceans that live concealed in the sea weeds, and there they are caught in the nets or are killed by the hunter, who comes upon them in his boat. Some-times they carve out wooden otters, paint them black, and set them afloat. The otter, seeing these images, swim up and indulge in various strange capers about them, and by this trick are caught. When they are caught in the nets they are so frantic that in their despair they bite off their frout feet, but if a male and a female are caught together they both lacerate their skins terribly and knock out their eyes.

We killed them on Bering Island with spears, nets, and, when they were lying asleep or in the act of copulating, with clubs.

They were found there in so great abundance that from the be-ginning our numbers did not suffice to kill them. They covered the shore in great droves, and as the animal is not migratory, but is born and bred there, they are so far from fearing man that they would come up to our fires and would not be driven away until, after many of them had been slain, they learned to know us and run. away. Nev-ertheless we killed upward of 800 of them, and if the narrow limits of the craft we constructed had permitted we should have killed three times as many.

As to the beauty of the animal, and particularly of its skin, this sea otter is alone incomparable, without a peer; it surpasses all other inhabitants of the vast ocean, and holds the first rank in point of beauty and softness of its fur.

As to its habits, it loves to live both in the water and on the land, but for the sake of sweet peace the otter inhabits in great droves, by preference, the great islands of the ocean. For getting food it seeks, when the tide is out, the shallow, rocky reefs overgrown with seaweed, and there devours crustaceans, mussels, clams, snails, limpets, polyps, cuttlefish. Only when forced by hunger to do so, do they eat seaweed, but they eat fish, smelt, and a little fish called in Kamchatkan idiom the "*Uiky*," which is washed in by the spring tides in countless numbers. They are also fond of meat, I have seen an otter eating the flesh of another otter which had been skinned and thrown away. It may therefore be concluded that this animal is omnivorous.

In the winter they lie some upon the ice, some upon the shore. In summer they go up the rivers and penetrate even to the lakes, where they greatly enjoy the fresh water. On warm days they seek the valleys and shady recesses of the mountains and frolic there like monkeys. They surpass all other amphibia in play and frolicsomeness, and in fleetness of foot.

On the land they lie, as dogs do, with the body curled up. As they come out of the sea, like dogs they shake off all the water before they lie down to sleep; then with their paws they wash their faces, just as cats do, smooth out their bodies, straighten out their fur, turn their head from one side to the other as they look themselves over, and seem to be greatly pleased with their personal appearance. I have also seen the males play with their genital organs like monkeys. When they are engaged in sleeking their fur they are so intent upon it that they can be killed readily.

A swift runner can scarcely overtake an otter when it runs, for it runs with many windings, in a fashion to mislead. When it sees its path to the sea intercepted and finds itself exhausted and out of breadth, it puts up its back like a cat, threatens to leap upon its pursuer, and spits like an angry cat, but we, being conscious that its anger was not dangerous, were not frightened off; and when it receives a vigorous blow upon the head it falls upon the ground, covers its eyes with its paws, and keeps them so, no matter how many times it is struck upon the back. But if one hits it on the tail, which is extended out as the animal runs, it turns about and faces the striker in the most absurd fashion. But more frequently it happens that they fall down at the first blow and pretend that they are dead, and then as soon as they see that we turn our attention to others they suddenly take to flight. From this it would appear that the animal is very cunning. Oftentimes we would drive them into narrow places on purpose, without any thought of doing them any harm; we would hold our clubs ready, and they would fall down fawning and looking around in every direction. Then they would slowly slink past us like dogs, and as soon as they saw that they were out of danger they would hurry with mighty leaps to the sea.

When they stand up they keep their necks extended in line with the body, and the hinder part, because of the length of the legs, stands higher.

They swim now upon the belly, now upon one side, and again flat upon the back; they also swim standing bolt upright in the water.

They play together, and, like human beings, embrace with their arms and kiss each other. If they escape the club, they gesticulate in a very ridiculous manner, as if making fun of the hunter. With one paw raised over their eyes, as if bothered by the rays of the sun, they watch the man, continually rubbing their pudenda as they lie upon their backs, and then go off into the water, still watching the man steadily and urinating as they go, in the same way as sea bears and whales also do.

They copulate at all seasons, and so throughout the year the mothers are seen busy with their cubs. Whether they give birth twice within one season I would not venture to decide; but I have seen, and I have sometimes killed, mothers with two cubs, one of which was a year old and the other three or four months old. So much is certain, they never, or at most very rarely, give birth to more than one at a time. The first year after they are born they do not copulate, but the second year they do. The period of gestation is eight or nine months; and so they bring forth perfectly developed young, with eyes open and with all their teeth; the four canine teeth are smaller than common, just as I have observed, also, in the case of the sea bears, seals, and sea lions.

They suckle their young almost a whole year. They preserve their conjugal affection most constantly, and the male does not serve more than one female. They live together both on sea and on laud. The 1-year-old cubs, the "*koschloki*," live with their parents until they set up housekeeping on their own score. Barely, therefore, are females seen apart from cubs two or three months old, which are called "*medviedki*."

The females always give birth to their young on land. Whether in the sea or on land, they carry their cubs in their mouths; but when they sleep at sea they fold their young in their arms just as mothers do their babes. They throw the young ones into the water to teach them to swim, and when tired out they bring them to shore again and kiss them just like human beings. They toss the young out into the sea and with their paws catch them when tossed, like a ball; and with them they engage in all the delightful and gentle games that a fond mother can play with her children. When the mother sleeps on shore the cubs keep watch, clinging to her dugs or arms. They embrace their young with an affection that is scarcely credible. When hunters press upon them, whether by land or by sea, they seize their young with their mouths and never let go of them except when compelled by extreme necessity or death itself. And so they are killed often when they might have got away themselves. I have sometimes deprived females of their young on purpose, sparing the mothers themselves, and they would weep over their affliction just like human beings. I once carried off two little ones alive, and the mothers followed me at a distance like dogs, calling to their young with a voice like the wailing of an infant; and when the young ones heard their mothers' voice they wailed, too. I sat down in the snow and the mothers came close up and stood ready to take the young ones from my hand if I should set them down in the snow. After eight days I returned to the same place and found one of the females at the spot where I had taken the young, bowed down with the deepest sorrow. Thus she lay, and I approached without any sign of flight on her part. Her skin hung loose, and she had grown so thin in that one week that there was nothing left but skin and bones. This happened several times in succession. It happened one other time that, in company with Mr. Plenisner, I saw in the distance a mother otter sleeping with a year-old cub. When she caught sight of us the mother ran to her offspring, woke him up, and warned him to flee; but, as he preferred to go on sleeping rather than to run away, she picked him up in her paws in spite of himself and rolled him like a stone down into the sea.

On land they can not see very well, but their sense of smell is very keen. They ought, therefore, to be hunted from the lee side. Their sense of hearing is just as sharp.

The cry of the sea otter is very like the cry of an infant. They doubtlessly live many years. They never breed strife among themselves, but always live on the best of terms with one another. They are very much afraid of sea lions and sea bears, and they do not like the company of seals. Accordingly the places which those animals frequent are carefully avoided by the otter.

The flesh of the adult otter is much more tender and savory than that of the seal. The flesh of the female is best, for it is fatter and more tender, and the fat lies between little membranes. It is for that reason a little hard. In the case of pregnant mothers, the nearer they are to parturition the fatter they are. In this respect they are different from land animals. The flesh of the young otter is most delicious; it can not easily be distinguished from the flesh of an unweaned lamb, whether roasted or boiled, and the gravy from its preparing, in either way, is most delicious. Otter flesh was our principal food on Bering Island; it was also our universal medicine. By its use we were saved from scurvy, and no one got sick of it, although we ate it every day half raw and without bread. The liver, heart, and kidneys tasted exactly like those of the calf. The natives of Kamchatka and the Kuril Islands give the first preference to the flesh of eagles, the second to otter's flesh. The liver and kidneys they eat raw, and declare them most excellent. Not only the natives but also the Russians use scrapings from the bony base of the penis as the proper remedy to cure the tertian fever.

The skins go through the following processes before they are ready for use. (1) After the skin has been taken from the animal shreds of muscle are cut from it with a knife. This process the Russians call by the Slavonic term, "bolon sniat." (2) Then the skin is stretched to its utmost; for, besides the fact that the price increases with the size, the skins thus prepared become lighter, although the fur does become less beautiful. (3) After this they straighten out the hairs with bones from the wings of gulls, and sleep upon them, naked, for several weeks to make them glossier, nicer, and more beautiful. This process the Russians call "*vyspat bobr.*" (4) While the Cossacks are getting the skins from the natives they frequently beat the skins upon the snow with sticks, and if the fur is gray, or any other color than black, they color them with alum and empetrum berries cooked to the proper consistency with fish oil. This makes them glossy black. But the frand can be detected — pull out of a dyed skin a single hair and it will show three colors: at the end, the black of the dye; from the middle down, the native color; and, finally, the base of the hair.

While the skins are being prepared for use, the natives treat them also as follows: they smear the inside of the skin with a powder made of dried fish eggs, as the Rutheni do with simple yeast; then they roll it up and lay it away for several days, and after that they scrape it with shells and glass, and finally smooth it down with pumice stone. During this time they knead the inside with a wooden hook and with the hands until it grows soft with the fermented dough of the fish eggs and all the fat disappears and the skin comes out soft and pliable. All other skins which are sold to traders are exported without any preparation, for it has been observed that these undressed skins keep their native color better.

I have wished to report about the sea otter what I have seen as an eye witness, and also what I have heard from the natives, in hunting them.

I have had two pictures made: Fig. 1 (Tab. XVI) represents an otter walking upon land, fig. 2 represents one swimming with her cub in the water.

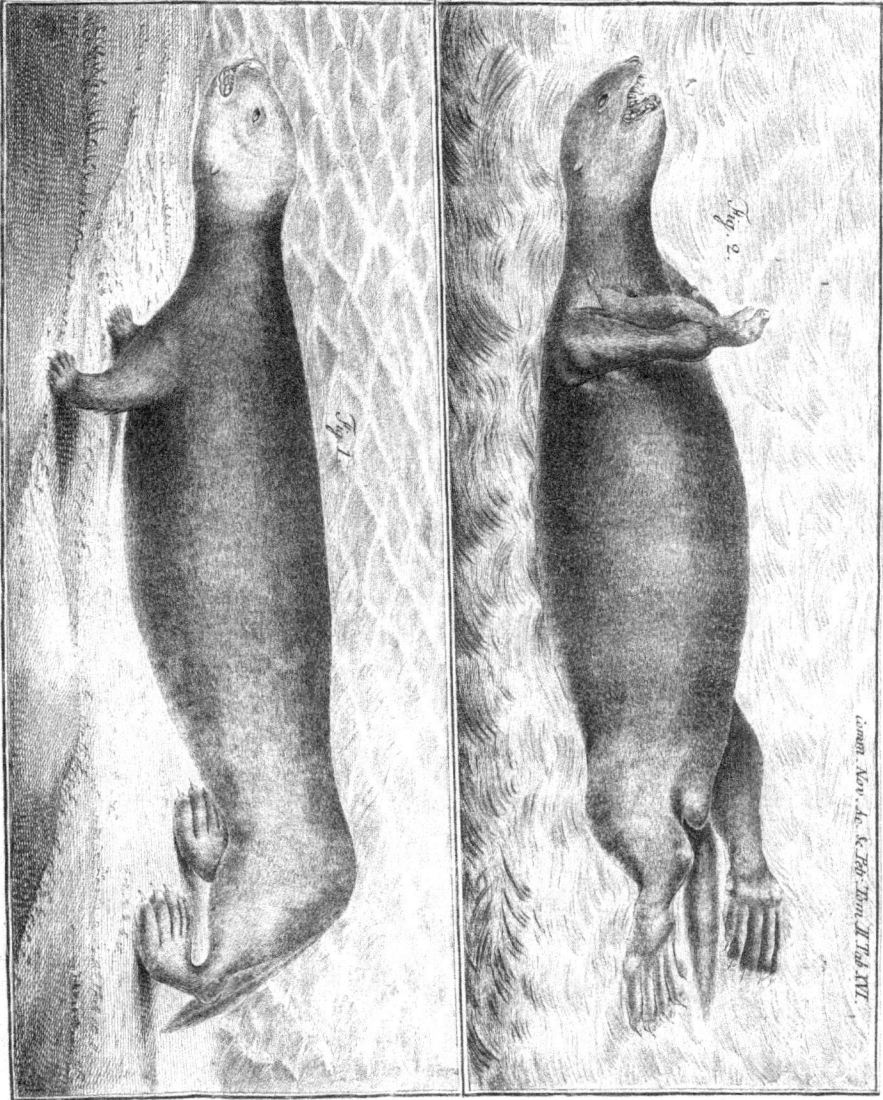

comm. Nov. Ac. Sc. Pet. Tom. II Tab XVI.

Appendix: Steller's Sea-Ape

August 10, 1741, Sunset, south of Kodiak Island

The animal was about two ells [six feet] long. The head was like a dog's head, the ears pointed and erect, and on the upper and lower lips on both sides whiskers hung down which made him look almost like a Chinaman. The eyes were large. The body was longish, round and fat, but gradually became thinner toward the tail; the skin was covered thickly with hair, grey on the back, reddish white on the belly, but in the water it seemed to be entirely red and cow-colored. The tail, which was equipped with fins, was divided in two parts, the upper fin being two times as long as the lower one, just like on sharks.

However, I was not a little surprised that I could perceive neither fore-feet, as in marine amphibians, nor fins in their place.

As for its body shape, for which there is no drawing, it corresponds in all respects to the picture that Gesner received from one of his correspondents and in his *Historia animalium* calls *Simia marina Danica*. At least our sea animal can by all rights be given this name because of both its resemblance to Gesner's *Simia* and its strange habits, quick movements, and playfulness.

For more than two hours it stayed with our ship, looking at us, one after the other, with admiration. It now and then came closer and often so close it could have been touched with a pole. Then, as soon as we moved, it retired away.

It raised itself out of the water up to one third its length, like a human being, and often remained in this position for several minutes.

After it had observed us for almost half an hour, it shot like an arrow under our ship and came out again on the other side, but passed back again to reappear in its previous position.

Now, when the animal spotted a large American seaweed, three to four fathoms long, which at the bottom was hallowed out like a bottle and from there to the outermost end became gradually more pointed like a phial, it shot toward it like an arrow, grabbed it in its mouth, and swam with it toward our vessel, and did such juggling tricks that one could not have asked for anything more comical from a monkey. Now and then it bit a piece off and ate it.

When I had observed it a long time, I had a gun loaded and fired at the animal, intending to get possession of it and make an accurate description. But the shot missed. Although it was somewhat frightened, it reappeared right away and approached our ship gradually.

But when another shot at it was in vain, or perhaps only slightly wounded it, it retreated into the sea and did not come back. However, it was seen at various times in different parts of the sea.

> Georg Steller, *Journal of a Voyage with Bering,* 1741-1742, O. Frost, editor, Margritt A. Engel, translator (Stanford University Press, 1988), pp. 82-83.

Johannes Kentmann, *Simia marina* (source of Gesner's picture in the *Historia animaliium* [1551-1587]).

Works by Georg Wilhelm Steller

Ausführliche Beschreibung von sonderbaren Meerthieren. Halle, 1753. (German edition of *De bestiis marinis.*)

Beschreibung von dem Lande Kamtschatka. Frankfurt, 1774. (English translation: *Steller's history of Kamchatka,* edited by Marvin W. Falk; translated by Margritt Engel and Karen Willmore. Fairbanks, AL, 2003.)

Journal of a Voyage with Bering 1741-1742. Edited by O. W. Frost; translated by Margritt A. Engel and O. W. Frost. Stanford, CA, 1988.

Observationes quaedam nidos et ova avium concernentes. In *Novi commentarii Academiae Scientiarvm Imperialis Petropolitanae, Tome* 4. St. Petersburg, 1758. http://www-gdz.sub.uni-goettingen.de/cgi-bin/digbib.cgi?PPN350423350

Observationes generales universam historiam piscium concernentes. In *Novi commentarii Academiae Scientiarvm Imperialis Petropolitanae, Tome* 3. St. Petersburg, 1753. http://www-gdz.sub.uni-goettingen.de/cgi-bin/digbib.cgi?PPN350411190

Reise von Kamtschatka nach Amerika mit dem Commandeur-capitan Bering. St. Petersburg, 1793.

Useful Links

Hans Rothauscher, Die Stellersche Seekuh (in German and English)
http://www.hans-rothauscher.de/steller/steller_d.htm

Sirenian International, Inc.
Fredericksburg, VA 22401 USA
http://www.sirenian.org/sirenians.html and
http://www.sirenian.org/stellers.html

Weinstein, B. and J. Patton. 2000. "Hydrodamalis gigas" (On-line),
Animal Diversity Web. http://animaldiversity.ummz.umich.edu/site/
accounts/information/Hydrodamalis_gigas.html.

Illustrations

Steller's field sketch and map

Steller's Sea Cow (*Hydrodamalis gigas*)

Photographs are from U.S. Fish & Wildlife Service Digital Library System.

Northern fur seal (*Callorhinus ursinus*)

Steller's Sea Lion (*Eumetopias jubatus*)

Photo: Forrest B. Lee

Photo: Tom Early

Sea Otter (*Enhydra lutris*)

www.ingramcontent.com/pod-product-compliance
Lightning Source LLC
Chambersburg PA
CBHW020008290326
41935CB00007B/344